Getting Unplugged

Getting Unplugged

Take Control of Your Family's Television, Video Game, and Computer Habits

Joan Anderson

Robin Wilkins

John Wiley & Sons, Inc.
New York • Chichester • Weinheim • Brisbane • Singapore • Toronto

This book is printed on acid-free paper. ∞

This publication is designed to provide accurate and authoritative information
in regard to the subject matter covered. It is sold with the understanding that
the publisher is not engaged in rendering professional services. If professional
advice or other expert assistance is required, the services of a competent professional person should be sought.

ISBN 0-471-17889-6

Printed in the United States of America

10 9 8 7 6 5 4 3 2 1

The primary danger of television lies not so much in the behavior it produces as the behavior it prevents.

—Urie Bronfenbremmer, quoted in Kenneth Kenniston, *All Our Children*

Contents

PART II: BREAKING THE HABIT

Chapter 5
THE FOUR-WEEK NO-TV PROGRAM 79

Chapter 6
KEEPING IT GOING WITH EQUAL-TIME ACTIVITIES 101

Chapter 7

Chapter 8

Bibliography

Index

Introduction

∿∿∿∿

THE WAY WE WERE

It was noontime. The kids were screaming for their peanut but-
ter and jelly sandwiches and I was racing around trying to get
lunch over with before my favorite soap came on. Groceries
were strewn everywhere as three-year-old Luke searched
through the bags for his favorite junk cereal. As usual, the television was blaring. Someone from McDonald's was telling us,
"We do it all for you." I remember thinking, *they don't do a
darn thing for me* when suddenly there was a loud crash. *Bang!*
I spun around, jelly dripping from my fingers, and there on the
floor lay our smoking color television set. In an instant we were
televisionless. Gone was the $500 item, the next episode of
General Hospital, and, worse still, the children's entertainment.

Poor Luke cried the loudest, as he was the one who tripped
over the cord and did the damage. Our older son, Andrew, and

I slouched down onto the kitchen floor, stunned. For a family that had Mr. Rogers' company at breakfast and *Entertainment Tonight* every evening, this was a crushing blow.

For a while we walked around in a daze. My husband was disgusted by our carelessness and refused to buy another set. In an effort to survive, we dragged out the old black-and-white portable but it proved dull and boring after years of color.

The loss of television was most devastating to me. It had taken so much effort to get the boys interested in *Sesame Street*. Neither of them had ever wanted to sit for very long, but I persevered, placing their little table and chairs near the set, giving them snacks to eat and toys to play with so they would stay put. Eventually my scheme worked: they became glued to the images before them, and I was free to get on with my day. Now, however, with the TV gone, I felt my freedom slipping away.

Life without television was an entirely new experience for the boys, however, and they rallied almost immediately, dragging their television table into the garage, where it became a tool bench. Our house, once melodic with Juicy Fruit gum ads and Kermit singing "It's not easy being green," now resounded with the sound of hammers hammering, doors slamming, and neighborhood children giggling.

"Hmmmmmm," I thought, "perhaps this was a blessing in disguise. Maybe there is life beyond television—and a better life at that."

Although at first the loss of our television made us feel as though good friends had moved away, it soon seemed that many new friends had moved in to take their place. We kept up with the news via radio, subscribed to a few extra magazines, began going to the movies, and frequented the local bookstores, where the boys chose one new book a week.

Looking back now, it seems as if we stopped mourning the loss of TV rather quickly, and within weeks we had decided not to buy a new one. In time, we did break down and buy a small color portable, which we used occasionally—but never again on a daily basis. Somehow we managed to live without television as our main source of relaxation, entertainment, and information, our exclusive window on the world. But that was more than twenty years ago. What about now?

THE WAY WE ARE NOW

The Wilkins family is certainly a part of the technology age. We now own two color television sets, a computer, and a good CD player. Although the boys are married and have moved away, when they do visit, certain televised events take precedence over family time. There are the professional football, basketball, and baseball games, each of which they insist is the most important game of the season. My husband disappears into our study for hours at a time to surf the Internet. Mercifully, without a VCR, we still have to leave the house to see a movie.

So how is it in the rest of the world? It doesn't take a genius to know most people are as hooked up as we are, if not more so. Walk around any neighborhood and you'll see the familiar glow of both TV and PC screens shining out of windows. In our area, three new video stores have opened in the past year. Everyone is wired for cable television, which now offers a hundred or more channels to lure us into more viewing. Many neighbors even have satellite dishes, and most people have access to the Internet.

Hooked-up houses are everywhere, and most of us now live inside a common electronic bubble, whether we live in New York or Alaska. Together we share a plethora of experiences, from gangster rap videos on MTV to simulated futuristic battles on the Internet; from docudramas about rape and incest to X-rated cable shows or videos.

And where once we only had to concern ourselves with the

effect of television on our lives, we now must consider the effects of computers, video games, interactive television, and more. When we should have taken technology more seriously, we flirted with it instead, and became infatuated with it and eventually addicted to it.

The job that today's parents face monitoring and controlling television and computer use by their children is mind-boggling. With preschoolers currently logging up to sixty hours a week in front of the television and adults sometimes watching more than that, where does an already busy parent begin?

The battle is not easily won because we have been subtly programmed to watch TV. Indeed, we've come to believe it is a necessary part of life. What's more, we're told every day that being technologically savvy is crucial. PCs are now standard homework equipment, the Internet is replacing the library, and video games are among the most popular forms of entertainment. Living in a hooked-up household is no longer a luxury but the norm. Startling as it may seem, we've arrived at Aldous Huxley's brave new world, where people depend on machines to reduce their thinking and where there is so much information coming at us through electronic media that we do not want or need to read books.

Author Richard Louv, in *Childhood's Future*, feels that television "is a thief of time. It has highjacked so many of our senses, so many parts of the brain that it leaves little room for self-generated images and ideas." Indeed, poet and humanist Robert Bly, as quoted in the Fall 1996 issue of *Utne Reader Magazine*, agrees: the tragedy of so much television is that "it is eating up more and more of childhood every year."

I don't think that any one of us means to be gobbled up by television. Instead, we want the family dinners, quiet moments, and time to relate to one another that are often sacrificed for more television time.

Still, we face a dilemma: to continue to give in to television and accept the idea that there's no turning back the clock, or to become sensible, not only about *what* we watch on television, but also *how much* television we watch and *how often* we watch it.

Our instincts tell us that we need balance, that a full life includes myriad experiences, that being alive means interaction with others, and that interaction with others grounds us and enables us to become more vital human beings. *Getting Unplugged* is for all parents who know better but find their children nevertheless seduced by television.

Just as we limit, control, and regulate everything else in our lives, so we need to strive to do the same with TV. *Getting Unplugged* will help you find balance in your life and create equal time for other important endeavors. It will help you understand how easily television can get out of control in all households; how it is possible and even reasonable to change your ways; and how and why making such a choice is good for your children and the entire family. We will explore what children need at various ages and stages, offer alternatives other than television and television-related activities, and finally offer a four-week plan that will help you break the habit. It's your life! Getting unplugged can only make it better.

THE PROBLEM
WITH BEING
PLUGGED IN

All the World's a Screen

~~~~~~

*I*t is 6:00 A.M. in Montclair, New Jersey. Ted Jones is working out on his treadmill while watching *Today's Business*. His wife, Joyce, is in the kitchen making breakfast with the company of CNN. When Ted rushes through the kitchen, grabs a mug of coffee, tucks his laptop under his arm, and leaves for work, he announces to Joyce that the children are behind schedule. Nine-year-old Tommy is watching cartoons and his older sister, Maggie, is revising her homework, oblivious to any confusion around her thanks to the music on her Walkman. Joyce leaves the kitchen to rally the kids at the first break in the news. The kids grab some breakfast on the run and finally Joyce is able to collapse at the kitchen table with the newspaper and a sweet roll. Thus ends another typical morning in a wired household where, from the first sound of their alarm clocks, each member of the Jones household moves through his or her routine independent of each other and to the accompaniment of each one's favorite electronic media.

MORNING MADNESS AND EVENING CHAOS

Today's home has been likened to a railway station, with parents and children pulling in and out at odd times. In fact, the only time many families regularly experience togetherness is when riding in the car or at home with the TV blaring in the background. The tie that binds the family together is often the television set, which, in a half-empty house, keeps parents and children alike occupied until other members appear on the scene, when, in all likelihood, they will continue watching together. "TV isn't just in the environment," wrote John Leonard of the *New York Times*. "It is the environment." Without even realizing it, we have allowed television to foster such a state of dependency that we can justly call it a national addiction.

THE BEGINNING OF THE VIDEO GENERATION

Our video culture has grown slowly, with electronic media subtly working their way into the social fabric until gradually television, video games, and computers have replaced good conversation with silence, fairy tales with sitcoms, and sitting by the fire with staring at a screen.

Most thirtysomething adults have never known and couldn't begin to conceive of life without television. The television they know is full of color, action, and shows that foster individualistic and antisocial behavior and values. But even in the fifties, when there were only three network channels and there was virtually no color, the standard black-and-white consoles seemed pretty exciting compared to radio and print. Most important, from the earliest days, the television industry has successfully made itself a part of everyday routines.

Consider, for example, how television watching has become part of the family dinner ritual. Dinnertime represents one of the few times during otherwise hectic days when parents, working parents in particular, can find a half hour of rest. The networks were quick to learn that if they hooked viewers while relaxing early in the evening, there was a good chance they would stay for the rest of the night. Accordingly, the evening news snagged viewers by offering excitement and drama as well as hard news. Today some of the most violent and sensationalistic stories appear on the news—not the nighttime series. In the 1960s and 1970s, families began buying television tables, foldable devices that allowed them to eat their meals in front of the set. Television tables, although not sponsored by the television industry itself, responded to and facilitated the industry's efforts to snare viewers—along with TV dinners, those quick frozen meals with all the courses in one pan that free up viewing time by eliminating preparation and cleanup. They represent the extent to which television had made itself a part of our daily lives.

Scholars and critics began raising red flags as far back as 1972. In that year the U.S. surgeon general ordered an in-depth study on television viewing. The resulting published report suggested too much television could be detrimental to children. At that time, statistics reported that children were watching six hours a day and up to fifty-four hours a week. A survey I conducted in suburban New York a few years later showed that most families owned three to five television sets, located in all of the primary areas of the home, including each bedroom, the kitchen, and the living room. The survey further showed that parents and children rarely viewed television together, and when asked if they would voluntarily give up television, the majority offered a resounding NO.

LIVING ON OVERLOAD

Today we find our lives saturated with a panoply of electronic gadgetry that we never could have expected or prepared for: family entertainment centers boasting TV screens with surround sound; personal private television sets for every member of the family; endless programming options with cable television; hip pocket technology that allows us to take our gadgets everywhere we go—from Walkmans and laptop computers to cellular phones, pocket-sized TVs, and video toys. Entertainment and information are readily accessible day and night, virtually at our fingertips, and we hold on to this access as desperately and habitually as a baby clutches a teddy bear.

> **❝** *Children respond well to quiet time. If the home is chaotic with television blaring, people shouting, telephone ringing, and people running in and out, the child cannot do anything but react in kind to the chaos.* **❞**
>
> —Dr. Benjamin Spock,
> *Rebuilding American
> Family Values*

We have been taught to believe television matters, that it is an important source for information, that every household needs television. And who has helped us believe this? The television industry itself, which spends billions of dollars providing us with shows that it advertises as significant and important.

In fact, in a frightening recent report from the Annenberg School of Communications at the University of Pennsylvania, three quarters of the parents polled believe that their children do not watch too much TV and that the majority of the programming does their children more good than harm, that television teaches and truly enhances their children's lives. Is this really the case? Perhaps it would help in coming to terms with the role of television in our lives if we asked ourselves one question.

WHAT IS TELEVISION?

Let's start by simply defining what makes television different from other forms of communication. According to Dorothy and Jerome Singer of Yale University's Television Research Center in their book, *The Parent's Guide: Use TV to Your Child's Advantage*, television possesses six specific properties that distinguish it from other media:

1. *Attention demand:* Continuous movement on the screen evokes an orienting response as the viewer focuses on the screen. Rapid movements and loud sounds activate the nervous system to a high degree.

2. *Brevity of sequences:* Interactions between or among people, events, and commercials are vivid and short.

3. *Interference effects:* The rapid succession of material prevents children from mentally repeating or reflecting on the new material to process and make sense of it.

4. *Complexity of presentation:* Several senses are simultaneously stimulated by the barrage of sights, sounds, and even printed words.

5. *Visual orientation:* Television is visually oriented and minimizes other sources of input.

6. *Emotional range:* Action presented is more vivid than in any other medium.

None of these factors is in itself bad. But it is important to remember that children think and learn on a different level than adults. Children haven't developed a capacity to distinguish fantasy from reality; they tend to interpret what they see on television very literally. This allows television to play three crucial roles in the lives of our children: salesperson, teacher, and companion—often with negative effects.

Television as Salesperson

Most of us are pretty skeptical about door-to-door salesmen. Now imagine if such a person came to your house when you weren't home and engaged your children in conversation, selling them ideas, thoughts, products, even a new way of life. Chances are if you walked in on such a scene you would kick the guy out, refute everything he said to your kids, and put *your* ideas in their heads instead.

Television's programs and advertisers, its information and spectacle, are all designed to deliver specific messages to the viewers about buying. The average child will view 350,000 television commercials by the time he or she graduates from high school, according to one study. The television industry is not in the business of selling programs to audiences. You've heard the phrase "This program is brought to you by such-and-such sponsor." Actually, the viewer is brought to the sponsor by the program. In other words, programming exists to sell commercials. In fact, commercial television is the business of selling audiences to advertisers. Issues of quality and responsibility are peripheral to the issue of maximizing audience. A decrease of just 1 percent in audience size, according to *TV Guide*, translates into a $250 million loss for the network! There are big stakes involved.

Trashy television is one of the ways the networks keep us hooked. By putting on show after show filled with sexual innuendos and references to body parts and bodily functions, networks are pulling out all stops to attract viewers, especially those with buying power. "We see how far we can go with the sex, violence, sensationalism, whatever it takes," said veteran television producer Don Ohlmeyer in a *TV Guide* interview, "and we are getting away with more and more. We need to deliver the general public to the advertisers. That's what pays our salaries."

"Most of us are being manipulated and influenced far more than we realize," said social researcher Vance Packard in *The Hidden Persuaders*. "Advertising is changing the very patterns of our lives. We think some of the commercials are fun and we laugh at them, but in fact these thirty-second blurps, complete with jingles and clever graphics, are reshaping our values, our desires, our very truth."

TURN-OFF TIP

Beware of Advertising Masquerading as Programming

Children have a significant influence over the purchase of products. Therefore advertisers circumvent parents, who may be more critical viewers and consumers, by bombarding our children with sales pitches. The children, in turn, bombard us with demands for the products advertised. In fact, some of the most popular children's shows were created primarily to feature preexisting toys. Rather than providing quality programming, these shows are actually thirty-minute commercials for action figures and other merchandise.

Children especially fall prey to the advertisers' hoaxes, as children are more readily enticed by images of explosions, weird cartoon figures, fascinating puppets, and the general kaleidoscope of visual imagery commercials offer. In addition, children more easily mistake slickness and expensive productions with credibility. In a recent poll, fifth- and sixth-graders believed the claims of 75 percent of all commercials. With such a gullible audience, it's no wonder more and more programming is aimed at the young viewer—who in time will become a major consumer. We've all seen children begging for certain toys and food in toy stores and supermarkets, often resulting in the immediate purchase of the product. What else is a busy parent to do?

In a free society anyone may sell whatever and however he or she wants. But how free are we, and our children, in the face of television's insidious role as salesperson? If we allow our children to be bombarded by the relentless and manipulative product-selling techniques of television from the time they are very young, will they ever develop the ability to resist a sales pitch? Or are we raising a society of consumers whose need to purchase cannot be separated from their need for visual stimulation, and who believe that both needs should be immediately satisfied?

Television as Teacher

When you think of television as teacher, your mind may automatically go to educational television. But all television serves the function of teacher, teaching our children values, points of view, and behaviors. Many of us choose a neighborhood to live in based on finding the best possible schools. We even try to negotiate with the building principal to handpick our children's teachers and often spend thousands of dollars on education, exposing our children through travel and cultural events to myriad other experiences. Even after such efforts, we remain curiously unaware that when they are not with real teachers or professors in schools and universities, they are being taught by a host of anonymous teachers who appear on television. These teachers, who come disguised as athletes, comedians, singers, and actors, teach our kids all types of values. Our children take in their points of view, bad or good, and spend more time with their television teachers than with the classroom ones we have researched and know.

As far as educational television is concerned, the television industry has done a good job convincing us that it is a vital teaching tool. Children watch only a third as much educational television as they do commercial TV, but we still hold on to the hope that any television offers them a window to the world.

As an occasional learning device television may prove handy, but children and adolescents need more. Television as teacher cannot be counted on to meet the mark because it does not offer any reciprocity. No emotions or feelings are exchanged, no questions asked or answered, and little time is made available for reflection. Learning, for all of us but especially the very young, must involve hands-on experimentation, exploration, action, and creative involvement. Since television requires only sight and hearing, we shut out a wide range of other sensibilities.

I remember when my sons were in Little League, how exciting those first few seasons were. But then I began to notice the kids dragging . . . they weren't running for pop flies, hitting as many home runs, or spending afternoons at the batting cages. I asked the coach what was going on. "They're watching the game on TV," he said, disgusted. "They're not playing it. They think that just by watching they will somehow turn into good ballplayers." Activity, including trial and error, is the hallmark of learning and growing. Little is accomplished by sitting and staring.

The famed psychoanalyst and observer of children Erik Erikson said in an interview with Joan Erikson, "Theory without action has no strength at all." When children are very young, it is vital to develop their physical, emotional, and intellectual systems. "Trying to hurry toddlers by sitting them down and introducing them to formal schooling can easily misfire," said the venerable Dr. Benjamin Spock in *Rebuilding*

TURN-OFF TIP

The Six Principles of Learning

Before you decide to use television as an educational tool, consider renowned educator John Holt's six principles of learning:

1. The task of adults is to support children in their learning.
2. Uninvited teaching is of dubious value.
3. Children learn from adult example.
4. Healthy children are curious and eager to explore the world.
5. Learning is rarely the product of teaching.
6. Giving too much help may destroy motivation, and unwanted interference may stop learning altogether.

Can television really provide a satisfactory and complete learning experience for your child?

American Family Values, "to say nothing of the sensory bombardment a child receives as he plays beside a turned-on television. All the imagery, color, noise only serves to get him to stop his play and stare, thus cutting out hundreds of moments of discovery and involvement."

It is true that *Sesame Street* and programs like it introduce toddlers to numbers and letters, but more than that, such programs introduce children to the habit of watching television. What's more, when we point them in that direction, we are giving children the idea that watching television is indeed good for them. And even educational television relies more on spectacle than it does on substance. It is chock-full of flash thoughts but stingy on philosophy, packed with visual images but weak on words, language, and ideas.

We've all had to deal with inarticulate teenagers who hem and haw as they speak. They seem to have a hard time putting together a simple sentence. Perhaps this is because they haven't practiced talking very much, having spent more of their time watching television, listening to music, and playing videos. But as media scholar Neil Postman said in *Amusing Ourselves to Death,* "Speech is an indispensable medium — it makes us human, keeps us human. Isn't it a shame that it isn't a more upheld value in our culture?"

I agree with the thought of educator John Holt as quoted in *Natural Childhood* that "uninvited teaching is of dubious value." We do ourselves a service when we carefully choose those programs we want for our children. When the specific program we've approved is over, we should turn off the television.

Television as Companion

After saying a quick hello to a parent or baby-sitter, most children run to the television or computer after school, and spend their afternoon with this companion who doesn't talk, ask questions, or demand any cooperation for hours.

One might wonder why children enjoy these nonhuman companions so much. Perhaps because the family programs on television frequently show siblings, parents, and neighbors involved in some kind of collective event that involves a whole group, each intertwined in the other's issue. Ironically, these TV families rarely sit passively and watch television; most of the time they appear to be having fun. Almost every show winds up with a warm and fuzzy conclusion that is emotionally gratifying to the viewer. Children get pleasure watching these fantasies of family life; some may dream of actually living this way.

Likewise, computers and video games offer entertainment when neighbors and friends are not around. With the capacity for interactivity, computers have the capability to perform as a real friend. Such simulated friendship is available after school and on weekends through the Internet. Kids can play sports, go on adventures, uncover treasures, fight battles with dragons, and communicate with others they will never see face to face via electronic mail.

But the computers and video games offers companionship without hassles, negotiations, or cooperation. Live friends, on the other hand, mean having to play fair, take turns, and understand the other; but for many children, simulated friends are becoming the preference.

Still, educators and psychologists believe that children need to be around real people. In "Is TV a Pied Piper?" the late Dorothy Cohen of the Bank Street College of Education in New York City said, "Children will not be fully human if they relate more to images than real people. All of society is slipping into a greater reliance on the image of the thing rather than the real thing itself. Television is no better or worse than the rest of society but it is the major instrument by which we hasten the process of alienation in our young and interfere with the process of ego strengthening, which grows primarily through contact with reality, not images . . . through participation and interaction with people and things, not through passivity and imitation."

Along the same lines, the Association of School Mistresses reports in "The Teaching of Reading," cited in *Television and Child Development*, "Children learn to speak by talking to other people, not by listening to mechanically reproduced speech. Real people speaking communicate the meaning of words, whereas television only reproduces sounds, a subtle but vital difference, confusing toddlers."

It is difficult to turn away from all the screens that pop up wherever we turn. We awaken, get dressed, go off to school and work, come home to eat and relax, and finally doze off, all with the help of various electronic media. And, although many of us can see the negative effects this dependency has on our children and their ability to fully develop, we turn away from the problem, thinking, *Why bother? How can I possibly fight something that is far bigger than I am?* Before you give up, let's discuss some real, concrete reasons why getting unplugged is crucial for your family.

Why Bother Getting Unplugged?

〰〰〰〰

Ｗe only get one shot at raising our kids, and all too soon they are grown and gone. Childhood is so fleeting, especially in this age of "the hurried child." In his book of the same name, David Elkind suggests that there has been a merging of the generations, with adults behaving more like children and children behaving more like adults. Technology has contributed to hurrying children along, and we can see and feel it in the way young children speak (often inappropriately), in their dress (often like little adults), and in their conversations (often far too serious, sarcastic, and full of anxiety). "There is so little downtime," observes a nursery school teacher in Massachusetts.

"Even at this young age, so many of the children in my school have few unprogrammed moments, little imaginary play, and almost no serendipitous discovery." We should always keep in mind that we are our child's first teacher. If we can make the most of this primary role, both our kids and we parents will reap tremendous rewards for the rest of our lives.

Guarding the formative years serves to guarantee that your child will have a reasonable chance to become a strong individual—his or her own person—particularly if you can find time to slow down and nurture your child's growth. No one knows what's best for a child better than his or her own parents. What's more, this knowledge is instinctive. "Most of the time, doing what comes naturally is exactly what our babies need," said Dr. Benjamin Spock in *Rebuilding American Family Values*, "whether it's cuddling, gazing into their eyes, rocking, talking, all the simple stimuli that helps the newborn along." We do not lose this instinctive sense of how to nurture our child just because he or she is no longer an infant, but sometimes we lose sight of its importance.

Advocates of the preservation of early childhood, such as Dr. T. Berry Brazelton and Dr. Elkind, emphasize keeping the early years uncomplicated and uncluttered. They encourage parents not to push their children, but to participate in their lives while encouraging self-discovery, imaginative play, interchange, sense experiences, and a connection to the real and natural world, all of which should come before introducing a child to television. In fact, these experts recommend that children under five watch no more than one hour a day. The issue of whether you allow your child to watch large amounts of television boils down to this question: How much do you value childhood itself? With little or no television in your child's life he or she stands a better chance to be more playful and alive, more invigorated by quality life, and even healthier, more fit and free. Such worthy goals are the aims of most parents, but too often our reliance on television interferes with our ability to achieve these values.

WHAT IT MEANS TO BE FULLY HUMAN

Becoming fully human means using all of our thinking, feeling, and sensing capabilities. "We do not need to teach children how to see. We can simply place the baby in an interesting and colorful environment and his sense of vision will go to work. Likewise, we do not need to teach him how to feel, but we can offer new things to touch and explore. The newborn's interest and curiosity in people and the world are already there, built in. And so it is with the other senses. The baby just needs us to offer the right opportunities," said Dr. Spock in *Rebuilding American Family Values.*

If a child's needs are so easily satisfied and his senses so naturally stimulated, what can he possibly get from a television that would develop his humanity? Some would argue that television provides early lessons in numbers and letters, or information about the world beyond a child's own small world, or stimulation from all the colors and sounds that come from the box.

❝ *Children must make meaning for themselves, instead of merely receiving it passively from external sources.* **❞**

—Jean Piaget, as quoted in John Thomson, *Natural Childhood*

Perhaps. But television only has the ability to engage two of the senses—seeing and hearing—and its doesn't do such a great job with vision. In his book *Amusing Ourselves to Death,* Neil Postman said, "The average length of a shot on network TV is 3.5 seconds, so the eye never rests, and there's always something new to see." To the child, especially a baby or toddler, this visual bombardment not only strains the eyes, which stay fixed, but also clutters up the entire sensory system.

While viewing, the eyes are defocused and motionless in order to take in the whole screen. Yet constant movement is required for healthy eye development. Visual exploration is necessary for developing a sense of depth and perspective; the two-dimensional screen does not facilitate such development. As a result, television viewing affects not only eye mechanics but also the ability to focus and pay attention. Why begin stunting your child's capacities and sensory development at an early age?

To get the most out of being human we need to continue to engage all of the senses to their full potential. Developing one sense without the others creates imbalance. Putting a baby to sleep in front of the television or leaving a two-year-old alone to experience fast-paced video imagery can have long-lasting effects. Children need to know how to effectively use sight and speech to elicit responses from people and in so doing have a chance for interactive relationships. But with its two-dimensional world of passive watching and listening, television deprives our children of that opportunity.

To Be Active and Playful

What else are children supposed to do? "Play is a child's most serious action," says French philosopher Montaigne. Child's play is his way of learning, where he achieves the necessary developmental tasks to grow and develop.

The repetitive play of a one-year-old is a way of developing sensory and physical mastery. The little one works hard to crawl, walk, and climb, and in doing so gets to know his own body's capabilities. Two- to five-year-olds' play consists of imitating parents and older children. They play dress-up and kitchen, taking on all the mannerisms of those around them, working hard to see the world from another's perspective. Hero play evolves as the child extends his boundaries and releases pent-up energy by playing princess, superhero, or astronaut. Imaginary play helps a child gain social skills as he acts out with little friends, gradually developing verbal skills and humor in the process.

❝ *Play must not be left to chance, for it is through play that the child learns and learns eagerly and with enjoyment.* **❞**

—F. Froebel, as quoted in John Thomson, *Natural Childhood*

TURN-OFF TIP

Eight Steps to Family Solidarity

By incorporating Dr. Spock's Eight Steps to Family Solidarity in our own families, we can provide balance, structure, and social awareness to our child's day.

1. Have family meals.
2. Have family meetings.
3. Have quiet time each day.
4. Participate in some kind of community service.
5. Participate in your children's school.
6. Make family recreation, vacations, and outings a priority.
7. Make things together as a family.
8. Limit television viewing.

When we encourage the use of television we stop the flow of expression, creative energy, and fun. "Whenever the child is given the notion that he needs to be entertained, learning comes almost to a halt," said Polly Berends in her book *Whole Parent, Whole Child* as quoted in John Thomson, *Natural Childhood.* When we point a child toward the television set we are in fact pointing him or her away from play.

The great gift we can give our children is permission, encouragement, and opportunities to *play.* Children will play games with whatever we provide, or make up their own games even if we don't provide them with anything. Children left to their own devices and with no television, radio, or electronic games will not sit and stare at the walls for very long. They will get on with another activity, for it is not in a child's nature to stagnate.

To Strive for Quality Life

According to the dictionary, *quality* is a striving toward excellence. Most parents would agree that reaching for a quality life by surrounding ourselves with beautiful things, incorporating high standards in our work, and exposing our children to valued ideas, people, and places is a worthy goal. Introducing quality into our children's lives begins when they are in the cradle and continues throughout childhood and adolescence. "If all children were cradled or rocked, held or sung to, or could just sit upon a lap and be read to once a day until they were six, we could revolutionize the world," said Dr. Viola Brady to a parent networking conference, as quoted in John Thomson, *Natural Childhood.*

How do we achieve quality in our homes? By providing soothing rhythms in the home, a pattern to every day, and practicing giving and sharing among family members. Quality in the home requires our presence, stability, attention, and advice, attitudes that allow everyone in the home to feel a sense of calm, safety, and warmth. Quality moments surface when all the senses can be engaged without interference and when opportunities for wonder and exploration are available to children and adults alike.

But today, with everyone in a hurry, it seems impossible to focus on achieving quality, so we reach outside ourselves to television programs and other things, hoping to buy quality or carve out a space for its existence in our cluttered lives.

I recently visited a school in Weymouth, Massachusetts, and questioned a group of veteran teachers about changes they observed in children over the past ten years. They all agreed that the children tend to be more sad and depressed than in the past. The consensus among the teachers was that the children needed parents to pay more attention to them, but the parents were always on the run. Many children in this middle-class area go home from school to an empty house, where, because of their parents' fear for their safety, they are required to stay inside and do little more than watch television or play Nintendo. "When I arrive at school in the morning," one teacher said, "I have several kids talking incessantly at me, so starved are they for real conversation."

More and more parents are finding it necessary to put their children in day care and pre-K programs and hope that with early socialization and stimulation their children will thrive. But one-on-one connection is the desire of most children. The famed educator John Dewey, as quoted in John Thomson, *Natural Childhood,* wrote that "only when we talk about and reflect upon experiences and information do we learn from them." For children to truly profit from any of their daily exposures they need time to think and wonder and then share with others what they have taken in. And when elementary school–age children themselves were asked in a recent Associated Press poll what they most desired (as reported in the

Cape Cod Times, October 1996), the majority had three wishes: more time with their parents; respect and encouragement from their parents for their abilities; and to be loved for who they are, not for what they do.

"Childhood is so brief, yet so open and informative," said poet Walter de la Mare in *Bells and Grass*. "Impressions are taken into maturity. I cannot believe that children, exposed to the best of literature, will later choose that which is cheap and demeaning. That is why only the best is good enough for children for whom we are shaping the future."

To Be Healthy and Fit

There is nothing more depressing than to walk into a room and see children slouched on a couch staring blankly at a screen while eating junk food. The only scene worse is watching the body language of a child (mostly boys) feverishly pressing a button to "kill the guy" and "finish him off" in a video game, either at a video arcade or at home in front of a television set or computer. One activity is as extreme as the other. Long periods of time at either end of the spectrum—passivity or aggression—are not good for children physically. Watching television does nothing for the body and is now cited by the American Academy of Pediatrics as the major reason why children have higher cholesterol levels.

A national health and nutrition survey conducted in 1994 and reported in Robert Durant, Tom Baronowski, and Maribeth Johnson in "The Relationship Among Television Watching, Physical Activity and Body Composition of Young Children," found that 4.7 million kids, ages six to seventeen, are severely overweight and that the main culprits are television viewing and high-calorie diets. According to pediatrician William Dietz of Tufts Medical School in "Children, Adolescents and Television," "The easiest way to reduce inactivity is to turn off the TV set. Almost anything else uses more energy than watching TV."

Similarly, playing video games in a darkened arcade with little or no exposure to daylight is also not a fit endeavor. "These children," reports a physical education teacher in South Weymouth, Massachusetts, "have done permanent damage to their wrists from hammering away on the video machine knobs. I've seen many such cases."

The same physical education teacher told me that 90 percent of the elementary school–age children he works with cannot score the maximum points in the President's Physical Fitness test. "Few score near the top," he said. "In fact, many of the kids are tired and out of breath long before their half-hour gym class is over. It's shocking. I blame it on too much sitting around."

In addition, one teacher reported that some children come to school restless and irritable after a late night of television viewing. A young growing body requires a period of sustained sleep without haunting dreams stimulated by the many inappropriate adult programs.

Beyond the physical side effects of sedentary behavior, another spin-off that comes with watching too much television and playing video games is internalized anxiety. A child's immature nervous system is particularly sensitive to stressors, and children have not yet developed skills for expressing unknown frustrations or releasing pent-up emotions healthfully. Could this be why attention deficit disorder is now found in epidemic proportions? And why there has been an increase in juvenile violence that has been widely recorded? If today's child sees some eight thousand murders on television by the time he is in sixth grade and witnesses two hundred thousand acts of violence and forty thousand murders by the time he graduates from high school, it is not unreasonable to conclude that the television and video games have had some contribution to the state of his or her mental and physical health. Balancing a child's day, maximizing his time in activity, outside, doing anything with motion, will only serve to create a more physically healthy human being.

TURN-OFF TIP

The Essential Needs of a Child

The essential needs of a child, as defined by Timothy Kahn in John Thomson, *Natural Childhood*, not surprisingly do not include watching television. In fact, time spent in the front of screens, whether televisions, computers, or video games, can take time away from fulfilling these essential needs.

What children need

- Food, warmth, exercise, sleep
- Love and a sense of belonging
- To explore, question, experience, and learn

What children need from us

- Listen to their ideas.
- Point out their achievements.
- Think through difficult situations with them.
  - Let them learn by their mistakes.
  - Make time for them.
  - Don't always tell them what to do.
  - Don't always tell them what they're doing wrong.

MAKING A CHOICE

It's far easier to keep a habit than to break one. Habits are comforting. They become part of our routine, and a day without one habit or another can feel strange, strained, empty. Most of us want to keep as much familiarity around as we can muster. But although we've been lulled and pacified by our television habit, a life of television addiction is a most unnatural life for a human being. Children and adults alike want to be actively engaged in a variety of activities simply for the feelings of excitement and personal satisfaction such activities yield. But now we are doing what the media are manipulating us to do rather than doing what we truly want to do

We all want our children to be free human beings. Encouraging them to seek other forms of expression, exercise, and experience will help them attain that goal.

To that end, ask yourself the following questions:

1. Have educators, psychologists, or philosophers ever suggested that it was important to watch television? yes/no

2. Does TV watching encourage good conversation? yes/no

3. Does TV watching encourage intellectual thought? yes/no

4. Are fake sights and sounds truly more gratifying than real ones? yes/no

5. Do we really need the latest electronic gadget? yes/no

6. Do television, video games, and the like enhance our lives substantially? yes/no

7. Can television and computers replace one-on-one interaction with real people, places, and things? yes/no

8. Is thirty minutes a day of quality time together enough for a parent and a child? yes/no

9. Do you make room for family time each day? yes/no

10. Is being overscheduled helpful to the development of your children? yes/no

11. Is a child's free-flowing dream time less valuable than planned activities? yes/no

Hopefully you answered "no" to most of the questions and can see the value of getting unplugged. Knowing what media do not do can be a motivating first step in limiting television's role in your family's life.

The Subtle Dangers of Television

*J*ust as it takes several months, even years to notice that you're gaining weight, so it also takes time for the effects of excessive television viewing to rear its ugly head. Television's harmful effects are not immediately visible or obvious, but eventually— and inevitably—problems develop.

WHEN DOES THE DANGER BEGIN?

Neil Postman contends in "TV's Disastrous Impact on Children" that "the medium of television becomes intelligible to children beginning at about thirty-six months. From this very early age television continuously exerts influence." Infants within earshot of a turned-on television set do not seem to notice or react particularly to the machine. But when these same children begin to utter sounds, their language may be garbled as they mimic the sounds that have characterized their environment—the sounds of television.

Later these children enter kindergarten with letter and number recognition already under their belts, courtesy of public television, and everyone applauds their head start. But around second and third grade, when asked to write words they know, string thoughts together, and think creatively and expansively, many of these children stumble, in part because they have only learned to understand pictures and words spoken by others. They haven't really done the hard work of absorbing the process of creating their own thoughts, stringing them together, putting them down on paper. When they become teenagers the residual effects become even more apparent. Many lack the ability to express themselves verbally, and when they do talk, their intonations and speech patterns mimic those of their favorite Hollywood and television characters.

I recently talked with a group of seventh graders in Phoenix, Arizona, who reported how much they *need* television and all of its accompanying background sound. "It makes it easier to talk when the TV is on," said one. "When it is silent you are forced to share thoughts and feelings. That's scary." Another said, "I like having television on all the time. It really does save you from awkward silences. We don't have dinner together very often but when we do it helps if the TV is on."

They all agreed that life would be strange without those television people and that television world. One young girl said that "TV has just pretty much become part of my life. It's there and I use it. Period." "It's not just background noise," another said. "TV is the main show."

DEFINING THE DANGERS OF TELEVISION

In 1977 Marie Winn's groundbreaking work *The Plug-In Drug,* which was based on interviews with middle-class families in New York and Denver, described in vivid detail the dangers of television. According to Winn, television has led to numerous crises, including a decline in reading and writing skills, a diminution of socializing experiences, fragmentation of the family, a rise in drug use, an increase in violent behavior, and the creation of a breed of remorseless children. Winn's findings have been confirmed by more recent studies as well.

In 1972 the surgeon general issued a report that concluded that television viewing had contributed to the disappearance of conversation and visits to friends' homes. Other apparent casualties were sleeping (heavy viewers sleep less), listening to the radio, reading, and eating dinner together as a family. An updated report conducted by the American Medical Association paints an even graver picture. In this report pediatricians responding to a poll blame exposure to television violence for heightened aggression in children, epileptic seizures (with video and arcade games being especially dangerous), nightmares, and injuries resulting from emulating dangerous television incidents. Fourteen percent of the responding physicians said they had seen children with behavioral and physical problems related to TV violence and to watching too much TV. Another 41 percent saw a connection between television watching, video games, and behavioral disorders, including the now rampant attention deficit disorder. As a result, many pediatricians are now taking a media history of their patients to consider the role of television when evaluating specific problems such as school performance, agitation, aggression, and problems with concentration.

Teachers, of course, see the disturbing symptoms long before anyone else, because they are with the children more consistently than even their own parents. I asked ten second-grade teachers to spell out the telltale clues that alert them to children who watch copious amounts of TV. Within minutes they offered the following:

1. Their language is overly mature, with sexual innuendo.

2. The boys frequently make sounds imitating automatic-weapons sound effects.

3. They're lethargic and inattentive and tend to terminate an activity before it is completed because they are too tired or bored to finish.

4. They're whiny and fussy when the others are still involved in their games or activities.

5. They have a limited worldview. They rarely refer to a book or a place or a museum they've gone to—TV programs are their only frame of reference.

6. They imitate their favorite television characters and exhibit little of their own unique personality.

7. They tend to be perfectionists. They are so used to the perfect graphics on television that they won't try a piece of art or music because it won't live up to the standards of television.

8. Their aspirations are little more than what television tells them they should be.

9. Television and programmed activities come first in their lives; schoolwork, second.

Several institutions and researchers have also studied the problem. Television research centers at Yale, Harvard, UCLA, and the Annenberg School of Communications at the University of Pennsylvania continue to measure and quantify television's effects. Joining them in the search for information and solutions are the National PTA, the American Medical

Association, and various religious organizations. Their observations and criticisms center on the following major areas in which television has a negative impact on our children:

- Weakened powers of imagination
- Exposure to sex and violence
- Confusion of real life with television life
- Extremely apathetic or overactive behavior
- Adoption of television values
- Interference with true learning

Weakened Powers of Imagination

All children need opportunities to make up their own images and use their imaginations. They need the chance to explore fantasy worlds of their own creation. Children who spend too much time in front of screens are being denied that right, and as a result they have lost some of their imaginative powers. Images come to them prepackaged, in color, and with sound effects. The child need only sit and absorb. The tragedy is that the children don't get to experience the hard work that occurs when they are forced to create mental pictures during the process of reading a book, listening to a tape or the radio, or playing with simple toys that don't have built-in images and sound effects. It was when reading books that children of yesteryear had to picture the witch or the hero, calling on their imaginations to do the job. We further dwarf our children's imagination by buying spin-off toys designed around television characters, video games, and other playthings that leave little for child's creativity to fill in.

Children need to learn that they are the source of their own activity, not television. Clocking hours in front of the TV creates an expectation that someone else should always be entertaining us.

A teacher of second graders tells me that many of her children have little or no initiative. "They are so heavily programmed with after-school activities and television that they are rarely left to their creative selves. As a result they don't seem to know how to take initiative."

A nursery school teacher at a private Waldorf School (where the philosophy is that children learn by doing, thinking, and playing) reports that those children who watch television have a hard time being creative during freeplay. "They usually stand on top of tables, draped in towels and aprons, and pretend to be one superhero or another. There is a lot of aimless running, punching, and shouting, and their references and speech patterns sound like a recording. Girls are especially skillful at mimicking TV characters." In another school I was told about a boy who thinks he is Bart Simpson, a popular cartoon character. "Truly, he speaks and acts just like Simpson," the teacher said. "I wouldn't want my own son to emulate such a gross character, but there it is. Nothing I do seems to be able to break him of this television character's traits."

A second-grade teacher in Denver is alarmed at how precocious some of her girls are. "They wear tiny shorts and midriff tops, striving for the MTV look." In talking to some sixth and seventh graders in the same school, one boy reported how strange his little brother's behavior is after a lot of television. "After watching the ninja turtles, he jumps up and wants me to see some move he's learned. And when he tries it out, he

❝ *Education is part of life, not separate from it.* **❞**

—John Dewey, as quoted in David Elkind, *Ties That Stress*

often falls and hurts himself. It's kind of sad." Another worried seventh-grade boy reports that his brother is into another show featuring cartoonish violence and martial arts: "That's all he watches and all he can play, and after the show he comes charging into my room and begins hitting me. He's actually bruised me!"

Children have always taken on the roles of their favorite heroes or characters in play. But close observers of heavy TV viewers say that these children aren't adding anything original or imaginative to their games. They know the television scripts by heart, having logged hours and hours of watching the shows, and simply repeat performances.

One of the saddest results of the proliferation of television is that some children have forgotten how to play altogether. A mother of two girls bemoaned her situation: "They sit and wait for their TV shows to begin while their toy closet stands untouched and neat. When they do play, their activity consists of jumping from one thing to another, making a huge mess, and then, after twenty minutes or so, walking away from the mayhem."

Many argue that television programs stimulate the imagination by exposing children to things they might not otherwise see or hear. But these programs demand very little of the viewer in terms of response or reaction. This lack of interaction while watching television is like eating a meal that is predigested. The child isn't even asked to chew.

Harvard University's Project Zero concluded that the method through which a person receives information makes a difference in how the brain is able to use it. Howard Gardner, the project director, states, "Television children rarely go beyond picture language either to pay attention to the audio portion or to connect TV experiences to their own real-life experiences." The project also found that children have better recall of stories read to them than stories seen on TV. It seems that children show a greater tendency to integrate their own experiences into a read story as well as to draw inferences from it.

Teachers concur. "I taught kindergarten before I taught second grade," said one, "and I have to say that both paying attention and using the imagination are down the tubes. I have found a way, however, to reach the children. I give them what they don't get at home or after school. I read them chapter books, books with no pictures, stories that are a reach for them. They are mesmerized. It's quiet time, and you can see they are thinking, picturing, reflecting. They love it! The imagination never dies, but I'm convinced we have to take blocks of time in order to reawaken or reinvigorate."

Exposure to Sex and Violence

Everyone has seen little children go "bang-bang" at each other and fall down dead when they are shot. These children have probably never witnessed a shooting—at least not in real life, but they have seen plenty of them on television. Psychologists believe that violence is a learned behavior, and studies have shown that children do indeed learn to be violent from television.

Of all the subtle dangers of television, the issues of violence and sex have been the most researched and well established. According to Brandon Centerwall, M.D., in "Television and Violence," when a child clocks twenty-five hours of TV a week, sees twelve thousand violent acts, hears fourteen thousand references to sex, and views a thousand rapes, murders, and robberies, his behavior, worldview, and fear quotient somehow will be affected. American television contains more violence than that found on the screens of any other Western country, and the amount of violent content, no matter how many laws have been passed to tone it down, has only increased over the years.

"If parents could buy a package of psychological influences to administer in regular doses to their children," said Albert Bandura, a Stanford University psychologist, in "Imitation of Film-Mediated Aggressive Models," "I doubt many would deliberately select Western gunslingers, hopped-up psychopaths, deranged sadists, and slapstick buffoons, unless they entertain rather peculiar ambitions for their growing offspring. Yet examples of such behavior are delivered in quantity to millions of households daily. As a result, today's youth are being raised on a heavy dosage of televised aggression and violence."

Recent prime-time programming is no exception. In the opening episode of one recent show, an unfortunate fellow is buried alive with his lips and eyes sewn shut; dialogue in a drama about a New York City vice squad is peppered with such words as *whore, ass, boobs, dyke,* and more. Study after study done by the surgeon general, the National Institute of Mental Health, and the American Academy of Pediatrics continue to report a significant link between heavy exposure to television violence and subsequent aggressive behavior. The basic reason for this is simple: Children model their behavior after adults, either the ones they see on television or the ones around them in real life. Since children often spend more time watching television characters than interacting with their own parents, it follows that today's child typical behavior could be becoming more violent and aggressive.

"Since I started teaching some twenty years ago," a teacher from Boston told me, "there is a huge difference in children's behavior. They are desensitized to violence. It is difficult for them to separate fantasy from reality. Several second-grade boys, for example, when asked how to solve a problem, suggested getting some dynamite and blowing the problem away. Poof!"

In Professor Bandura's classic 1963 experiments with nursery school children and a Bobo doll (a punching bag with a sand base and a red nose that squeaks), children in the control group were separated from the experimental group, and the experimental group was shown a short videotape.

The tape begins with an adult male walking up to the Bobo doll and ordering him to clear the way. When the doll doesn't move, the man punches him in the nose, raises the doll and pummels it on the head, and shouts "Stay down!" and "Pow, right in the nose!" while kicking the doll and throwing balls at it. After seeing the tape the children were given a similar doll, and they all proceeded to treat it precisely as they saw it being treated on television. The group that did *not* see the tape, when given the doll played with it in a nonviolent way.

Everywhere one looks today there is confusion between the confected and the real, between images on a screen and real life. More and more life has come to resemble entertainment. Before he blew up the federal building in Oklahoma City, convicted bomber Timothy McVeigh reportedly rented *Blown Away*, a movie about a former IRA terrorist baiting an old colleague who is now on the bomb squad of the Boston police.

The American Psychological Association summarizes the effects of seeing violence on television this way:

- Children become less sensitive to the pain and suffering of others.

- Children may be more fearful of the world around them.

- Children may be more likely to behave in aggressive ways in most situations.

How does television violence differ from the violence in traditional fairy tales, which are filled with gory incidents and terrifying villains? For one thing, most children view television while they are alone. Their parents or baby-sitters are often in another part of the house, while monsters, murderers, and various other brutes entertain the child. The child takes in the fear but has no way to channel his or her anxiety. A fairy tale, on the other hand, is usually read to a youngster while he or she is sitting on Mom or Dad's lap, secure and safe. When there is a scary moment, it is cloaked in the warmth of a parent's voice. Questions can be answered, fear can be talked through, and most importantly, there is communication between two human beings. "Ever since I can remember," said an eighth-grade girl, "my little brother has been watching TV alone. No one ever tells him he can't watch something. But then he gets scared at night and sometimes can't sleep."

A psychologist from the University of British Columbia discovered an isolated town in Canada that was about to receive television for the first time. Knowing it was the last chance to measure behavior changes before and after the arrival of TV, she rushed to analyze the schoolchildren, then returned two years later to measure the effects of television. "We found significant increases in physical and verbal aggression," she reported.

❝ *Many kids become depressed or have nightmares because of the barrage of bloodshed they see on TV.* **❞**

—Hillary Clinton, *It Takes a Village*

As Mrs. Clinton points our in *It Takes A Village*, television numbs children to the pain and destructiveness of actual violence, encouraging a stance of ironic detatchment. Television contributes to what George Gerber has identified as the "mean world syndrome," where children internalize the negative attributes of the world as portrayed in the media.

Confusion of Real Life with Television Life

At a New York Council for Children's Television meeting, teachers reported that first, second, and third graders assume much of what they see on TV to be real and true. One teacher reported that the children in her class were upset for weeks after seeing *Jurassic Park*, a film she had recommended. The teacher's intention of introducing dinosaurs as part of the curriculum was overshadowed by the violence of the prehistoric animals ravaging some of the film's characters.

When my own son Luke was seven years old, unbeknownst to me he watched the TV movie *Salem's Lot* and shortly thereafter refused to go to bed without the light on in the bedroom, bathroom, and hallway. One day I asked both our boys if there was anything they were really afraid of. "Oh, yes," Luke piped up, "I'm scared of Barlow." "Who's Barlow?" I asked. "The vampire on *Salem's Lot*," he answered. "That's why I'm afraid to go to sleep at night."

Children need parents to explain the mysteries that a television box holds for them. Children's fears come alive at bedtime, and many are a direct result of television. One preschooler I met was afraid to go to sleep because she thought the "green eyes" would get her. Her mother took all the steps that comfort children. She looked under the bed, in the closet, and inside the drawers, declaring that no green eyes were to be found. But the child persevered. "Yes, Mommy, the green eyes are in the box." "What box?" her mother asked. "The television box," answered her daughter. The child had seen a commercial for a horror movie in which there was a witch with green eyes; quite naturally this five-year-old thought that all the creatures on the screen lived in the box.

A little boy in upstate New York was watching a war movie one day that featured a chase scene with World War II planes. Suddenly his mother heard a loud crash. She ran into the room to see her son standing next to a broken television screen.

The boy looked up dazed and explained that he only wanted to see where the airplanes had gone.

Unfortunately, it is all too easy for our children to believe that reality is what they see on television. And television and video games create a reality that is sometimes meaner and scarier than the real world.

Extremely Apathetic or Overactive Behavior

Perhaps the worst time of the week for parents is Saturday morning, when Mommy tries to coax Johnny away from cartoons and get him outdoors to play. She calls him several times, but to no avail. Finally, in frustration, she shouts, "Johnny, turn off that TV!" Johnny slowly turns in her direction, tries to focus his glazed eyes, and answers, "Do I have to?" An angry conversation follows, with Johnny becoming more cranky and miserable by the minute. Clearly no one is going to win at this game.

Part of the problem may be that Johnny has been jarred out of an alpha state; his brain waves as he watches television are in a pattern that indicates deep relaxation. According to a study for General Electric by sociologist Herbert Krugman titled "Brain Waves Measures of Media Involvement," after a very short span of time (sometimes as few as thirty seconds) a television watcher's brain waves go into an alpha pattern. In other words, when a child is called away from the TV after a heavy dose of viewing, he or she is being awakened from a pseudo-nap in which his or her "dreams" have consisted of the ingredients dished up in the shows he or she is watching—noise, ugly and frightening characters, frantic music, violence. It should come as no surprise, then, to find that on most Saturday mornings you have a grouchy and irritable child.

At the other extreme, some children are simply overstimulated after being bombarded by all of television's sensory impressions. Dr. Werner Halpern of Rochester Mental Health Clinic reported in "Turned-On Toddlers" a sudden increase in the number of two-year-olds being referred to him for behavioral problems. They were restless, hyperactive, frantic, and sometimes exhibited other problems, such as inappropriate speech that contained a great deal of compulsive serializing of numbers and letters. These children found it easier to relate to things than to people. A battery of tests revealed that the children were not psychotic, autistic, or schizophrenic. Dr. Halpern concluded that watching television, particularly *Sesame Street,* was the one thing all of the children were exposed to. When the children stopped watching television, their symptoms disappeared and their behavior improved rapidly.

The problem isn't just about programming; it's that being "programmed," being glued to the tube, is an unnatural activity for young children who need to be active and interactive.

Another simple reason for the overactive child might be that it is not natural for active, young human beings to stay in a sitting position, staring at a box for hours. When the television goes off after several hours of watching, children are bound to be wild, loud, and busy; they have a whole untapped well of energy. They simply need to make up for the time spent being idle and contained.

Adoption of Television Values

Not only is television affecting behavior; it is also affecting values. For centuries children have received their values primarily from their families. But television has changed all that by stripping us of old-fashioned rituals, traditions, and values and replacing such personal birthrights with a more homogenized variety dictated largely by television. I recently conducted a no-TV week in a school at the beginning of December. When the children became aware that they could not watch television, they were devastated. "What about *Frosty the Snowman?*" they asked, "or watching *Rudolph?*" For many of them TV specials were an integral part of what was significant about the holiday (along with the presents they begged for as dictated by the commercials they had ingested). After the no-TV week began, however, they settled most happily into activities that were not television-related, traditional activities many of them had never done: candle-dipping, decorating cookies, making gingerbread houses and ornaments for the tree.

The most popular people on TV are very attractive and usually have money. The less attractive and poor are often ridiculed and shunned. Jim Bougas, a history teacher in Massachusetts, explains how values are being shaped by the tube: He cites a Diet Pepsi commercial in which a popular female model, dressed in cut-off shorts, drives a Lamborghini into a backwater Texas town, gets out of the car, walks to a Pepsi machine, and gulps a Pepsi down to the beat of rock music while two young boys watch, mouths wide open, and then say: "What a beautiful car."

"I try to teach seventh and eighth graders to look at such commercials with an analytical perspective," said Jim Bougas, "in order to get them to think about how their thought processes are being shaped by TV. Because so many young people are seeing fifteen-second soundbites and twenty-minute shows with eight minutes worth of commercials, they are not thinking in depth anymore and instead making conclusions and forming values based on soundbites."

Children begin to believe that they, too, must be rich and beautiful to be liked. What's more, they see so many sex scenes on TV that they believe such behavior is normal even at young ages, and as a result are having sex earlier than any previous generation. Commercials show that buying advertised products will make the buyer look like the actor in the commercial, and children believe that if they buy a certain product they, too, will find success.

An impressionable young viewer is quite likely to take these video values for his own. A 1982 National Institute of Mental Health report by David Pearl, *Television and Behavior: Ten Years of Scientific Progress and Implications for the '80s*, stresses the role of television as a powerful and persuasive educator that has become a major "socializing agent" of America's young.

66 *We're strip mining our children's minds and doing it for commercial profit.* 99

—Al Gore, quoted by Brian Burke @btburkeacep.org.

Teachers at a nursery school in Englewood, New Jersey, report that when they ask the children what they did over the weekend, most children describe not fun activities, but the programs they watched. Even with additional prodding and probing, most children find it difficult to remember other events. Perhaps they went to church, visited Grandma, or went to the grocery store, but all these activities fade when compared with television activity.

"So thoroughly has television saturated the environment we make and share with one another," said television critic Rose Goldsen in *The Show and Tell Machine*, citing work of psychologists H. R. Beech and H. J. Eysenck, "that nearly every child born in this country is inescapably immersed in its symbols during the formative years. What will happen to body movement and rhythms of these children, their facial expressions, their emotive use of language, their dreams, their fancies, and their fantasies? Will all converge toward some universal mean? What are the symbols that will call forth their allegiance, devotion, and reverential love?

Interference with True Learning

Teachers across the country report dramatic changes in the manner in which they must teach to reach the television child. In an interview with the author, Sheila Nielsen, a second-grade teacher at a Waldorf School in Spring Valley, New York, spoke of children's brains being programmed to seven-minute time slots. "Because most programs run for seven minutes and then break for commercial, children are programmed only to concentrate for that length of time." These children are not able to immerse themselves in absorbing thought. They have learned to listen for just a set amount of time and then change channels! Many teachers have learned to adapt their lesson plans accordingly so as not to lose the child's interest.

"No question about it," said another second-grade teacher in the same school. "The children have a quick-fix mentality. They're used to immediate gratification, and it makes their attention problems, or lack of attention, all the keener."

Dr. Mary Alice White, a professor of psychology at Teachers College in New York, cites the same problem in the fall 1981 issue of *TC Today:* "By the time the children are three and four years old, they have learned that music and sound effects, and sometimes changes in types of voices, are cues to make them look at the television screen. They come to school with a set of strategies they have learned from the electronic system that do not apply to the classroom setting. I don't think they know when to listen."

One teacher interviewed believed it was necessary for preschoolers to develop vocabulary and language skills so they would be ready to move on to the more difficult skill of reading. Several teachers in Boston note that in the past ten years children's vocabularies have dwindled and are full of nonsense jargon, their conversations peppered with goofy slapstick. "A typical child learns about three thousand new words a year, and the majority of new words are learned while reading," said Diane Robinson, a third-grade teacher. "Since children are reading less, it comes as no surprise that the written vocabulary of the average child has shrunk from twenty-five thousand words to ten thousand words in less than fifty years," she said. "Imagine if parents limited TV watching, how their children's vocabulary would be enriched. Parents are giving ample opportunities for their children to view television, videos, and play Nintendo, but where are the opportunities to read?"

The *Cleveland Plain Dealer* queried several veteran teachers on the effects of TV and learning and came up with depressing answers. "The past ten years have been tough," one teacher said. "The kids challenge me about their tasks. They're disrespectful and have less self-control and they're coming to school with so much anger," said Larry Mumford, a fifth-grade teacher who has been in the profession since 1964. He blames TV for disrupting children's attention spans. "Kids have changed, and TV is the culprit."

"We can't present material the way we did twenty years ago," said Beverly Chambers, a twenty-one-year veteran of the Cleveland school system. "Their attention span and the influences on them make them different people. Their speech is full of profanity and they're rude. Things they should have learned at home, the teachers now have to teach."

Do they need educational television? Is any kind of television helpful in the schools? There are two schools of thought on educational shows such as *Sesame Street*. As written by Hillary Clinton in *It Takes a Village*, a University of Kansas study conducted by John Wright and Aletha Huston showed that children who regularly watched *Sesame Street* were better prepared for school and performed better on verbal and math tests. However, those children who consistently watched noneducational TV and adult programming scored lower on the same exams. A Children's Television Workshop study over a three-year period followed low-income children and found that if they watched *Sesame Street* as early as two years old they would perform better on tests than if they had not watched.

Sesame Street's original intention was to reach low-income children so they might be ready for the task at hand when they reached kindergarten. The methods designed to reach them were modeled after the TV commercial. By selling letters and numbers the way television sells toothpaste and toys, the creators of *Sesame Street* hoped to reach their audience. No one could have predicted that *Sesame Street* would take off in such a phenomenal way. In fact, it was never intended to be watched as it currently is, nor was the format designed for children under age three.

Now we have supersophisticated children (not disadvantaged, but often *over*advantaged) geared to learning, and used to being continually and explosively bombarded with television techniques in the process. Such children show problem signs from taking in so many sensory impressions. "Rapid changes and choppiness of movement prevent reflection on the part of the child," said Werner Halpern in "Turned-On Toddlers." "This kind of learning is destructive because it hinders a child's adaptive capacity and disturbs the balance of the child's inner life. Overloading the sensory receptors breeds a sense of powerlessness. There are children who cannot deal with many new sensory impressions all at once, and *Sesame Street* provides neither the time nor the repetition children need to reflect on stimuli, thereby digesting and truly learning the material." Since Dr. Halpern's report, the producers of *Sesame Street* have slowed down portions to increase the learning opportunities of their young viewers.

Jerome and Dorothy Singer, a Yale University husband-and-wife team who head a television research center, find that children benefit more from slow-paced programs: "*Mr. Rogers' Neighborhood* allows children time to savor the material," they say in "Is Human Imagination Going Down the Tube?" "We have found that after viewing Mr. Rogers for a few weeks, children become more imaginative and cooperative. They smile and concentrate more than the child who has watched *Sesame Street* for the same period of time."

The Importance of Reading

The consensus among authorities, researchers, teachers, and psychologists is that nothing can replace a good book for children's learning. Even the best of television can't beat a book or magazine because books are read at the pace of the person reading it. There is no way to stop a television program and ask a question. In a book a child can go back to his favorite page and look at it again. Hillary Clinton, in her book *It Takes a Village*, says, "When parents read or talk to their children during the first three years of life there is a strong foundation for future reading success. That is why nurses and doctors have begun to prescribe reading to babies along with regular checkups and vaccinations."

Mrs. Clinton continues to speak of one-on-one contact in an essay for *Newsweek* magazine. "In today's high-tech world it is easy to forget the importance of human connections in our daily activities. Reading to a child, while hugging, touching, and holding him or her on our lap can be a wonderful antidote to the impersonal tendencies of our information age. While critical to building brains, reading is equally important to building trusting and close relationships. If Americans take away only one lesson from this exciting scientific age it is that reading to children is easy, affordable, and feasible no matter what their level of education or economic status in life."

Reading is the essential ticket to learning, but learning to read should not be a race. It doesn't matter when your child starts to read as long as the endeavor is enjoyable. The parents'

TURN-OFF TIP

Teachers' Rules

Here are some rules elementary school teachers would like to make for the parents of their students:

1. Allow no television on school nights.

2. Make children accountable for their tasks in the evening. Empty their backpacks and look for instructions from the teachers.

3. Have more conversation with kids. When they come home they have so much to say and want to tell their parents about their day.

4. Participate in a no-TV week if for no other reason than the fact that these weeks force parents to spend more time doing something else with their kids than watching TV.

5. Limit the time your kids watch TV. Children actually want appropriate boundaries and limits.

6. Make bedtime eight or eight-thirty for all elementary school–age children. They need more sleep than most parents realize.

7. Allow no television watching before school.

job is not to teach a child to read but rather to help the child along by reading to him or her and listening when a child starts to pretend to read a book.

Even computer whiz Bill Gates admits that books are a crucial educational tool. "Books are great," he said. "You can put them in a crib, kids can take them on a bus or a plane, they will continue to be very important. Still, I see computer software replacing books on occasion, and such programs will offer surprises and discoveries that books cannot. Fortunately books and hardware work hand in hand. My kids will have computers, of course. But they will have books first."

Several teachers in South Weymouth, Massachusetts, bemoaned the fact that interest in reading has diminished. "The kids watch far more television shows and play video games instead of reading," said several teachers. "If only we could get across to parents that reading is everything. In the past ten years reading at home has all but diminished. We try to encourage parents to take their children to the library . . . that everybody take out a book and read together in the evening, so that children will know the feeling of curling up with a good book and want to do it the rest of their lives." Here are some further tips:

- Build up a collection of interesting books.

- Read to your children while they look at the pictures. In time they will anticipate the phrases and start reading themselves.

- Let your child set the pace of reading, and choose a time to read that suits your child.

- Let your child make mistakes without constantly interrupting. Most children go back and correct their own errors.

- If your child asks for help, give a clue without actually giving a word. Just as adults skip words they are not familiar with and work out meaning from context, children do the same.

Computers and Video Games: Two Sides of the Chip

*I*t was only after thirty years of television watching that we came to recognize the problems of television addiction. While computers are relatively new to the school setting and only just beginning to become a fixture in most homes, we might do ourselves a favor by considering potential problems now before it is too late.

THE PROBLEM WITH COMPUTERS

Marie Winn, in her book *The Plug-In Drug,* asserts that machines (be they computers or television) put into the hands of children too soon may deter children's ability to:

1. Develop capacities for self-direction in order to liberate themselves from dependency. Machines perpetuate passivity.

2. Develop fundamental skills in communication—reading, writing, and expression—in order to function as social critics. The computer experience does not further verbal development.

3. Discover their own strengths and weaknesses in order to find fulfillment. Playing on a computer limits such discovery.

4. Satisfy their fantasies and be gratified far better by their own make-believe activities rather than those programmed on the computer.

For young children the computer creates a dependency on the machine rather than oneself, when having confidence in one's own abilities should come first. Later, after the child has developed his or her own thinking and analytic abilities, the computer can enhance the child's sense of those abilities. The key is that computers should enhance the learning experience rather than become the sole source of learning.

The present preoccupation with computers may result in children losing the ability to initiate, to communicate, and to produce unless prompted by a machine. A mother whose son has a special aptitude for computers is worried. "My concern about Ben's development as a human being goes beyond whether he will think too linearly or that somehow computer literacy will affect his approach to other problems. I want him to interact with other people in a positive way, to stay in touch with his own needs as a human being, to be able to reach out to others, and to feel good about himself. Because no matter what he does in his life, these are the sources of happiness."

But with today's children exhibiting short attention spans, declining oral and written skills, troubled social relationships, and poor listening skills—problems that can be linked to the use of visual electronic media—it is worth considering keeping them from the computer for those all-important preschool years, at least, and managing their computer use throughout childhood. Educators who believe strongly in Jean Piaget's philosophy of learning, which involves action and reflection time in order for children to absorb what they're doing, assert that steps can't be skipped in a child's mental and physical growth. You can rush the stages, the seasons, by putting children in front of machines such as computers, electronic games, and televisions too early in life, which in the end may hamper their growth. Current brain research adds to Piaget's ideas by suggesting that all visual electronic media contribute to actual changes in children's brains, changes that negatively impact the ability to process information—that is, to learn and to think.

Physical effects aside, as Ben's mother noticed, a computer cannot offer real-life contact with people, ideas, and things. What I hear over and over again from teachers is that kids are hungry for personal interaction. They want someone who will sit down and play with them. Playing alone on a machine, no matter how brilliant its responses, still leaves a child essentially alone. No matter how creative the computer program, the child presses a key and artificial images appear—not real life. Furthermore, there is little room to explore possibilities that have no readily visible results. Granted, this shortcut to a desired outcome has appeal, but the process of learning is every bit as important as the end product.

Dr. David Elkind contends in his book *Miseducation: Preschoolers at Risk* that the introduction of computers into the home has been so rapid that no one knows what impact they will have on mental development and academic achievement. "Some see the computer as a powerful tool, enhancing intellectual potential; others see the computer as just another technological tool that enables one to work more efficiently."

When asked if four-year-olds should be introduced to computers, Dr. Elkind replied: "Only if they are really interested. You might show them how pressing keys results in a picture on the screen, or how you can write his name and print it out. If he isn't interested in this, don't pursue it. Insisting when your child is not ready serves to deter his interest down the line. Working with a computer," Elkind continues, "is far different than working with live objects, people and the environment. In fact right now, the computer is sufficiently complex that to operate one well, a person must have a fairly high level of mental development. Complex machines are not easily understood by young children."

It is important to note that, like introducing your child to reading, foreign languages, sports, or artistic instruction at an early age, early computer literacy is not guaranteed to launch your child onto some royal road of success. The computer does not improve a child's ability to remember any more than television does. And these electronic media should never take the place of real objects in the preschool setting, such as picture books, dolls, dress-up clothing, and bright

❝ If you want your children to be brilliant, tell them fairy tales. If you want them to be very brilliant, tell them even more fairy tales. ❞

—Albert Einstein, as quoted by John Thompson in *Natural Childhood*

toys. Computers may fascinate, even bring information, but they don't teach.

The U.S. Department of Education commissioned a survey in 1987 and found no evidence to indicate that schoolwide test scores had been affected by the kind of computer use that occurs in elementary school settings. Computers in the elementary schools, the study revealed, were there primarily to acquaint students and teachers with the new cultural object. They had not affected students' learning in math and language in any significant way.

Software developer and former grade-school teacher Tom Snyder believes schools are imposing computers on children and teachers and driving both deeper into isolation. Snyder is angry at educators as they buy up software designed to replace teaching. "The computer thus far has done little that is educationally significant. What it has done is capture our imagination and prompt us to to finance possibly the biggest unfocused research effort in the world," said Snyder, as quoted by Richard Louv in *Childhood's Future*.

"Sixty percent of the software used in education is drill-and-practice—and most of it is never used once it gets into the classroom," continued Snyder. "When it is used, it is used by one child, sitting in front of a screen, alone."

SOCIAL PROBLEMS CAUSED BY COMPUTERS

Although we may want to keep from technologizing our children, many kids already prefer their computers to real-life friends. "You don't have to take turns," said one sixth grader. "And I don't have to be fair." Another said, "It is easier to get along with my computer because it doesn't explode at me and get angry like my dad does." Some third and fourth graders told me that "the computer doesn't get hostile."

"Yeah!" said another. "It doesn't jump back at me. One of the games I play on the computer, the program says mean things to me and I can shout back. That's fun!"

One little girl told me she liked playing with her laptop better than her dad because it doesn't fall asleep on her. This same child comes home to an empty house and finds her computer keeping her company. "I'm not lonely when it's on." Another little girl said her computer gives her independence. "I can do things all by myself and don't need to ask for help," she said proudly. "Plus it gets me away from my little sister."

Still, we don't want computers to isolate children one from another. "Some really bright kids get hooked on information," one teacher commented about the Internet. "I try to stay on the lookout for these kids so they don't get 'zoned out' and 'sucked in.' When I spot such a child I ask him to keep a list of where his surfing took him, how far afloat he went. This way he can begin to see just how much time he has spent and maybe wasted." This same teacher admits to doing a lot of surfing himself on the Internet. "It's very addictive and time-consuming," he said, "eating up hours I could have spent at the gym, taking advanced courses at the local community college, or just being with friends."

COMPUTERS AND EDUCATION

The computer industry is selling the idea that very young children need to be computer literate, if for no other reason than computer companies need to sell their ever-changing models, parts, and software.

And schools are gobbling up computers and their accessories, believing the hype. Hardware sales to schools alone are a billion-dollar business. Most school systems think the ideal is to have a computer on each student's desk. Some futurists envision that computers will replace desks, wall-size computer displays will replace overhead projectors, and students will be able to access any book in the Library of Congress at the touch of the button.

The tragedy of all this thinking, according to Tom Snyder, is that software designers basically don't understand that homes and schools are supposed to be human places. "We don't listen to what teachers have to say, we don't ask them what kids need. I don't care if my kid ever touches a computer in school," he continues. "If my kid loves his teacher, that's what counts."

School curricula have become increasingly tied to textbook publishers' ideas of what children should learn, and now the same thing is happening with computers. It really does boil down to big business. According to the Yonkers, New York, Consumers' Union, commercial pressures have penetrated U.S. classrooms, leaving kids as "captive audiences" and "consumers in training," as reported by Amy Aidman in "Advertising in the Schools: Selling America's Kids."

Peggy Cole, retired principal of the Fieldstone Lower School in Riverdale, New York, and an outspoken critic of television for the young child, also questions the appropriateness of computers in the schools. As quoted by Sally Reed in the April 25, 1982, *New York Times* spring survey of education, Ms. Cole says, "This movement of getting computers into every classroom is not coming from an education base, but from industry. There is the seduction of technology, tremendous parental pressures, and a business motive. What is missing are solid educational reasons for doing it at all. Questions have to be asked first. For example, if you put something into the curriculum, what are you going to take out? We usually introduce children to the concrete world in first and second grade before the abstract world. What will it mean to introduce them to the symbolic world first? What about the graphics on computers? Aren't they just as distorting to a child as cartoons?"

There's no question that all people in the future will need

to understand how to work computers. But so much of the technology will be outdated by the time today's school-age children have entered the workforce that it might be counterproductive to devote so much classroom time to mastering something that will be obsolete.

In fact, some computer specialists even suggest that early training may handicap young kids because it requires them to "unlearn" the primitive ways. Furthermore, they will still have to start from scratch as new models and forms of the computer appear. "One of the problems with the whole industry," said Massachusetts computer specialist and teacher Charles Corkum in an interview with the author, "is that there is always the new, bigger, and better part. The average consumer can never catch up."

So the question is, why use valuable developmental time becoming acquainted with today's computer when the young child might better involve himself with hands-on activities?

There is nothing wrong with introducing computers in early childhood education, if they are introduced as fun machines that can enhance or supplement reading, writing, and math skills. But the operative word is *enhance* or *supplement*, not substitute for books, writing, and one-on-one interaction with a teacher. Computer-assisted instruction as a tutoring method for five-year-olds practicing the alphabet and number recognition can become a playful activity, and educators report favorable results. Furthermore, children don't complain when they have to do the work over and over again. But computer programming, computer-generated art, and word processing are best left to older children in the fourth, fifth, and sixth grades, after they have mastered writing, drawing, and math skills on their own.

"Let's not forgot the importance of such things as writing skills," said a teacher from Boston. "When words are punched into a keyboard they come out letter-perfect. But actually writing words is a process of manipulation as the child guides the pencil into a shape or form. Even the most sophisticated mouse is distinctly different from pen in hand."

Computers are a valuable tool, enriching the resources a school district makes available to students. However, the key ingredient to any curriculum supported with technology is age-appropriate software.

Perhaps the greatest danger presented by the computer is the diminishing influence of the teacher. "History has shown that teaching devices, when introduced into education, have marginal influence," report William Sharkan and John Goodman. "There is no instructional technology that can substitute completely for a teacher who is a real person—one who has developed an adequate and positive self-concept, who has a system of values, who genuinely likes kids, and who has the desire to teach."

Education is an intensely personal human process. Communication between students and teachers will always involve a great deal more than does the interaction between kids and computers.

THE WORTH OF COMPUTERS

Computer teacher and expert Charles Corkum said in an interview with the author, "Computer games, puzzles, and creative environments are stimulants for transforming mental actions such as comparing, organizing, and symbolizing in young children." In this sense, he feels computer learning is active learning.

Indeed, a computer's saving grace when compared to a television is that a computer is interactive, it demands participation, and it is *not* a one-way source of communication.

To the delight of many parents, television watching is declining dramatically when children have a PC available to them. And these kids aren't just dropping television in favor of computer games. Parents report that 60 percent of their child's computer time is used to write papers and explore information. They also like to collaborate on computer projects with their sisters and brothers.

Teachers warn, however, that computers should be introduced first as a source of information before the game pattern sets in. "If the students only know the machine for the games they can play on it, it is my experience that they will not turn to it for anything else," said Charles Corkum.

But even computer games are not useless in moderation. "Computer games are not as trivial as one might think," said an elementary school principal. "For it can be such games that motivate children to learn more about computers, while also learning to use the mouse, thus enhancing eye/hand coordination and reasoning skills at the same time."

"I must admit that little kids love the computer as a drawing tool," Charles Corkum said. "They are dazzled by all the colors, and it teaches them numbers and reading. After all, they have to read the letters on the keyboard to create words on the screen. I've had good success with third graders at keyboarding and math skills. I think that's a good introductory age."

"As a direct primary source for middle schoolers, you can't beat it," said Steve Forest, teacher and media specialist at the Phoenix Country Day School, in an interview with the author. "One of my students did an interview with a leader in Peru right after the embassy crisis. Another boy interested in karate was able to pull up all kinds of color photographs, graphics, everything relating to the sport. It's like looking at one of those well-stocked magazine racks that has something for everyone."

At a recent panel on rearing children in the electronic age, one panelist suggested how a computer might be used in class. "Children can plot simulated pioneer trips across country in a covered wagon, programming all the hardships a family might encounter along the way." Children understand computers because they can control them. Many of the most inquisitive and self-motivated students are drawn to computers. But still many of the panelists suggested hands-on activities that could make the same point and make it more compelling than the computer. One panel member mentioned that during deer season a father had brought into school a deer that the children skinned, dried, and stretched, using the experience as part of a pioneer unit they were working on at the time. None of this could have been done on the computer.

THE INFAMOUS INTERNET

Created in the late 1960s to protect defense data from nuclear attack, the Internet is a worldwide network of computer networks. It is the center lane of the so-called information superhighway. This electronic superhighway provides users with the opportunity to enter a world commonly known as "cyberspace." In cyberspace, ideas can be exchanged, research information can be accessed, jobs can be found, and educational information can be explored. Research suggests that the use of electronic networking can help teachers and children reduce a sense of isolationism, connect with peers across the country, and increase the power of both cooperative and independent study.

The most powerful features of the Internet are electronic mail, discussion groups, data bases, and the World Wide Web. For example, electronic mail enables school groups and individuals to compose, send, and receive messages with their peers. Students can also be part of national discussion groups focusing on topics in their curriculum, such as space exploration and the environment. World Wide Web sites offer graphics and links to materials housed in a variety of places on the Internet.

One of the benefits of the Internet is easy access to the vast resources in the world's great libraries—a benefit no one ever could have imagined a generation ago. To be able to retrieve information from the Library of Congress enables young students to access highly specialized information.

But the Internet can become a potentially negative force in the life of the young child. For some youngsters, being on the Internet is an excuse to lose themselves in another world. The Internet is an outlet for freedom of speech in the broadest sense. As a consequence, some youngsters may find themselves in areas that portray sex and violence in a way that many parents would deem inappropriate. Pornography has proven to be a problem in open networks such as the Internet and cable. At a slumber party for nine-year-old girls the host mother was shocked to find the children staring at a pornographic movie in the middle of the night. Similarly, the Internet has been known to lure unsuspecting children toward dangerous situations. One such example was a young man who was lured to Seattle, where he was confronted by a pedophile. At a private school in New York City, a ten-year-old boy found himself exposed to a file on a computer screen filled with ten thumbnail-sized pictures showing couples in various acts of sodomy, heterosexual intercourse, and lesbian sex.

Parents must exercise caution in monitoring their children's use of the Internet. Software has been developed to prevent children from breaking into adult arenas, but open access to certain chat rooms without parental supervision may bring unsuspecting youngsters into contact with undesirable computer partners.

VIDEO GAMES

Outside of educational uses, children enjoy their computers as an at-home video arcade, but parents must think carefully about whether to allow children to play computer games. There are claims that these games develop dexterity and quick thinking, but there are also claims that it is better for children to develop these abilities through sports and exercise. In addition, many computer games are high in violent and sexist content. In a study conducted in the United States, it was found that 72 percent of Nintendo games belonged to the violent category. Even the sports games surveyed were found to have a certain vitriolic quality. Most home video games stress autonomous action rather than cooperation: A common game scenario is that of an anonymous character performing an aggressive act against an anonymous enemy. "The individual in a video game is alone working against an evil force. The world of video games has little sense of community and few team players," complains a nursery school teacher in Massachusetts.

Even so, video games continue to be a popular pastime for children. It seems apparent that video games, whether handheld, on computers, or at an arcade, would never have taken off in such a phenomenal way if they had not been tailor-made for the children of television. Children gravitate to video machines if for no other reason than familiarity; children feel comfortable with them because they are once again dealing with animated, on-screen images.

Several single parents I know are thrilled that their children now have something to interact with when they come home to an empty house after school. "These machines are far more imaginative than television," said one excited father. But video games, like television, are an isolating experience. A visit to any video arcade confirms this. The lights are dim, the kids are serious, and the customers stand with their backs to one another, hands hammering away in a frenetic motion at knobs and buttons. Most striking is the observation that players of video games have the same dull look in their eyes as heavy television watchers.

The most popular video games are those that deal with the martial arts and other violent themes. The most preferred games are those that involve fantasy violence. Some of the more popular titles have names such as *Mortal Kombat, Total Carnage,* and *Street Fighter.* The objective is to kill or maim the opponent by any means necessary. According to Parker Page, psychologist and president of Children's Television Resource and Education Center, as quoted by Dr. Benjamin Spock in *Rebuilding American Family Values,* "It looks like some kids who have a steady diet of playing violent video games may be more at risk of being more aggressive with other children in the real world or more tolerant of aggression around them." They are also desensitized to violence, much like the television-addicted child.

According to Jeanne B. Funk of the Department of Pediatrics Medical College of Toledo, Ohio, some reports indicate that video game playing triggers epileptic seizures in a small group of susceptible children. In fact, one of the manufacturers of handheld video games has issued a warning on its game as to the possibility of this outcome.

"Many video games simply encourage a sense of perversity and brutality," wrote Dr. Spock. "The player takes on the role of characters like Captain Carnage and Major Mayhem whose predominant goal is to gauge, smash, shoot, or vaporize the opponent." One such game features a muscular man and a well-developed woman in various cops and robbers shoot-outs, urging players to attack the enemy with automatic rifles, machine guns, grenades, and explosives. Another includes overdeveloped, tattooed males with shotguns killing similarly ugly characters. The female is dressed in skimpy leather under-wear, and she whips the other characters. The winner is the one who kills the most people. "These games are not going to make killers out of kids," wrote Dr. Spock. "But large doses of vicarious violence conditions them to accept real violence as one of the solutions to life's problems."

When pushed for an answer as to why video arcades are so attractive to children, especially to boys, many arcade workers say that these machines are a replacement for loneliness. "Some boys who come in here feel that the arcade is their home," remarked one manager. Several boys I talked with in a video game parlor told me that they feel powerful and in control while playing the games. One boy confessed, "When I'm depressed and angry about something that happened at school, I can come here and shoot away rather than blowing up my history teacher."

Psychiatrists are beginning to see game-fixated youngsters, and they report that for the most part these are disturbed children who dodge reality and human contact. My nephew's sole source of conversation is the plot of a computer game. He is five and plays with these games (both on the computer and the handheld variety) during most of his spare time. As a result, much of his language, references, and stories stem from the characters in the games he plays. Arcade managers say that their establishments have "regulars," boys who come daily in hopes of increasing their score and thereby being able to place their initials on the video screen of their particular game. Some boys are so addicted they spend upward of twenty dollars a day.

The children most hooked on video games are those with few interests. They don't play sports. They don't participate in extracurricular activities. They actually derive self-esteem from video games. According to Robert Jackson, a computer expert and teacher at the Meade School in Westchester, New York, as quoted by Joan Anderson Wilkins in *Breaking the TV Habit*, "Children with short attention spans who are unteachable in most normal school settings can be turned on somewhat by playing with video games and simple computers." Yet, on the other side of the coin, according to one special-education teacher from Massachusetts, "You have the children with perseverance who do one thing over and over again. These children are extremely hard to break of computer game playing yet they are the ones in need of more creative activity."

But not all video games are negative. Some can have a positive effect on children. There is an entire business dedicated to developing more challenging and interesting software. Some are dedicated to developing software to explore different places in the environment. "Computer games can give children intellectual confidence and increase motivational levels," wrote Erna Fishhaut, in her article *Video Games: A Problem or a Blessing?* "Many computer games promote a feeling of mastery," she said. "If parents choose a game or program wisely it can enhance their child's learning."

Because of the still-limited research regarding video games, parents should act conservatively. One mother I talked to held off buying Nintendo for several years. When it finally appeared one Christmas morning, it was played with for a time, but then her son gradually lost interest.

When I asked a group of fourth graders about video games, most of them had already come to the conclusion that the games are pretty stupid. "I used to love SuperNintendo," said one boy. "That's all I used to do, but then I'd just get tired." Another said, "After an hour the game is boring." When asked if they were given eighty dollars would they spend it on a computer game or something else, it was unanimous. "Something else!" The key for us, as adults, is to provide them with alternatives. Otherwise, no matter how boring it may be, they will still gravitate to the familiarity and comfort of their electronic diversions.

Video games are no different from TV. Enjoy them in moderation. Perhaps these kids have found the perfect natural solution. If we can deemphasize the role computers and video games play in our lives, if we can temper our own addictions to electronic media, then maybe our children will naturally gravitate to healthier activities.

Breaking

the

Habit

The Four-Week No-TV Program

"*O*kay, okay, I get the picture," you may be saying. "But how do I change not only my TV habits but also those of the rest of the family?"

The Four-Week No-TV Program I will describe has been adapted from the no-TV weeks I have conducted in elementary schools and parent workshops. You and your family can try it alone, or get together with other families in your community in undertaking the program. In fact, no-TV weeks have been organized and are a fixture in many elementary schools throughout the country. The Four-Week No-TV Program is a process of gradual withdrawal from television designed to make all family members aware of their television viewing habits and to help each person see the opportunities for enrichment and exciting activities that will fill his or her day when television is no longer a constant.

THE TV DIET

Abusing television use is just like eating or smoking too much. You're not going to go on a rigorous diet unless you truly feel unhappy with your flabby thighs, tight waistband, or popped buttons. You won't try to stop smoking until begins to affect your health, when you find yourself huffing and puffing after a simple walk up a flight of stairs or gasping for breath on a tennis court. Then and only then will most of us take action.

So it is with the overuse of television. But surely you've had more than a few guilt pangs when you find your children staring at the box when they could be outside on a sunny day. More guilt when you've organized your day around your soap opera schedule . . . or as you listen to the hum of different programs coming out of various bedrooms at night . . . or when a televised sporting event keeps you or your spouse from being really present at one of the children's birthday parties.

Denial plays a big part in keeping you from taking action. To face the music, we've devised a TV quiz to help you 'fess up to your addiction as well as that of the rest of your family. Have everyone in the family take the test and then compare scores. (There are similar tests in the back of the book should you want to check your video game, computer, and video use.)

THE TV QUIZ

1. How many television sets do you own?   _____

2. Where are the sets located?
Living room . . . Bedrooms . . .
Kitchen . . . Family room   _____

3. How many hours a day do you watch? _____

4. How many hours of TV does each child watch? _____

5. Do you/they watch TV alone or with others? Alone . . . With others . . . Both _____

6. Do you/they watch TV because you are bored or have nothing else to do? Yes . . . No _____

7. Do you/they turn off a show that doesn't interest you? Yes . . . No . . . Sometimes _____

8. Does your set(s) remain on for long periods of time, or even when you or your children are not watching? Yes . . . No . . . Sometimes _____

9. Do you/they watch TV in bed at night? Yes . . . No . . . Sometimes _____

10. Is TV on during meals? Yes . . . No . . . Sometimes _____

11. Do you turn off the set when someone drops in? Yes . . . No _____

12. Do certain shows have an emotional effect on you/them? Yes . . . No . . . Sometimes _____

13. Do you turn on the set to entertain your preschoolers? Yes . . . No . . . Sometimes _____

14. Do you rent videos to entertain preschoolers? Yes . . . No . . . Sometimes _____

15. Do you watch TV mainly to relax?
Yes . . . No . . . Sometimes   _____

16. Would you miss TV if you didn't have
a set? Yes . . . No   _____

How to Score Your TV Watching

1. 5 points for each set
2. 5 points for each room
3. 1 point for each hour
4. 1 point for each hour divided by the number of children
5. Alone, 5; Others, 2; Both, 3
6. Yes, 5; No, 2
7. Yes, 0; No, 5; Sometimes, 3
8. Yes, 5; No, 0; Sometimes, 3
9. Yes, 5; No, 0; Sometimes, 3
10. Yes, 5; No, 0; Sometimes, 3
11. Yes, 0; No, 5
12. Yes, 5; No, 2; Sometimes, 3
13. Yes, 5; No, 0; Sometimes, 3
14. Yes, 5; No, 2; Sometimes, 3
15. Yes, 5; No, 2
16. Yes, 5; No, 0

How to Interpret the TV Quiz

A score of 90 or above indicates that there is too much television in your life and you should get your habit under control. If you scored from 75 to 90 you are a borderline TV addict and should take steps to curb your viewing. Under 70 indicates you have a television conscience and probably don't need any help controlling your viewing habits.

Don't be surprised if you scored over 85. Ninety percent of those who have taken this test score well over 85, and there is no reason your family should be any different. Remember, television was *designed* to entice, electrify, and entertain, so it's really not your fault that it has wormed its way into your life.

However, after reading the symptoms and dangers of television addiction, it is your fault if you allow you and your family to continue to be held by television's power. It's time to get unplugged and begin to control your television instead of the other way around.

With your newly developed consciousness, you know what must be done: Turn off the TV and turn on your body and brain. It's time to speak up to yourself and speak back to the TV. How to start?

WEEK ONE: WATCH YOURSELF WATCH

Begin the first week right in front of your screens so you can actually clock the number of hours you and the other family members watch. Your only task will be to keep track of your normal daily schedule. Fill in the daily time chart (at the end of this section), recording all activities, including television programs and videos watched, and video games played. At week's end total the number of hours spent in front of the screens.

Do a separate chart for each family member who cannot do it for himself or herself, encouraging any children who can to keep their own charts. The process is a real eye-opener, especially for mothers who have little time to account for their children's TV habits.

The entire family should participate. Your household will have an "experimentlike" ambience that will help launch your anti-TV campaign in an upbeat, cooperative way.

TURN-OFF TIP

Post this notice in a prominent spot in your home for added encouragement.

Six Reasons Why Your Children Need to Break the TV Habit

1. Children must learn to live their own lives before they learn about the lives of others on television.

2. Your child needs to emerge as his or her own person in the early years of life, not as a pretaped version of a TV child.

3. It is not in a child's nature to be unhappy. Without TV, your child may be temporarily bored, but soon he or she will develop a path of happy, active living.

4. We must not lose the art of childhood. Our culture needs active, imaginative children who will keep fantasy and play alive

5. Why supply children with a pseudo–life experience when their natural instinct is to create their own experiences?

6. Children want to relate to people most of all, not machines.

While watching your favorite shows, count the commercials in any given hour. Be aware of the violent acts and total them up as well. Finally, list some of the products advertised during these programs and look around your kitchen, bathroom, and laundry room to see how much TV has affected your family as consumers.

DAILY TIME CHART

	Sun.	Mon.	Tues.	Wed.	Thurs.	Fri.	Sat.
6 A.M.							
7 A.M.							
8 A.M.							
9 A.M.							
10 A.M.							
11 A.M.							
12 P.M.							
1 P.M.							
2 P.M.							
3 P.M.							
4 P.M.							
5 P.M.							
6 P.M.							
7 P.M.							
8 P.M.							
9 P.M.							
10 P.M.							
11 P.M.							

Total TV Hours:
Total TV hours watched this week:

TURN-OFF TIP

How Much TV Is the Right Amount?

Here are some helpful hints from the American Academy of Pediatrics and the Department of Education.

While there is no "right" amount of TV-watching time for children, the thirty-five hours or more a week that many kids spend in front of the TV is clearly excessive. In your household, zero might be the right amount on weekdays. In your neighbor's house, an hour or hour and a half each weekday might feel right. We recommend not more than *two hours per day,* including weekends.

To arrive at a rough guideline for yourself, use this TV value equation:

1. Compute the amount of time between the end of school and bedtime.

2. Subtract time for schoolwork, extracurricular activities, snacks, dinner, bedtime preparations, and other must-dos.

3. Decide what percentage of your child's remaining discretionary time would be well spent in front of the TV. Define "well spent" in terms of educational content, the quality of entertainment, the offering of good values, etc. Convert the percentage into hours and minutes. What's the number? How does it compare with actual screen time in your home? Maybe it's time for a change.

WEEK TWO: TAKE A CRITICAL LOOK

Continue television watching but start viewing more critically, asking questions such as, Why am I watching? Why did I suggest the children watch? Do we need the evening news, or should we have dinner in peace and quiet instead? Would I rather be outside or watching my soap? Try to decide at the beginning of each day which programs you intend to watch and why. After watching each show or video, rate it: excellent, good, fair, or poor.

Factors to be taken into consideration when watching both television or videos:

Quality of the Script: Is the situation realistic? Are the jokes funny? Do the characters act like real people? Is the dialogue of high quality? How did the program make you feel?

Extent of Violence: Was the violence on the program necessary? Did it scare you? Was it appropriate for children's viewing?

Degree of Honesty: Did the story really answer the questions it raised? In the case of a documentary, was the subject dealt with comprehensively? Could the story happen in real life?

Entertainment: Was the program worth the time you spent watching it? How would you have solved the problem you saw on the show? Did you simply like watching it? Was it a good escape?

Use the accompanying program chart to assist you in your critical viewing. Children may need help filling in the chart. Consider setting aside an hour each evening when you fill in your charts together and discuss each other's ratings. At the end of the week each of you should ask the following questions:

- How many shows did I watch this week?

- Did I watch more or less than usual?

- If I decided not to watch TV, what did I replace it with?

- What other activities did I include in the week for entertainment, relaxation, information, companionship?

PROGRAM CHART

Choose from the following for your reason for watching a particular show:

Entertainment, Pleasure, Relaxation, Nothing Else to Do, Information, Other

Choose from the following for your rating of each show:

Excellent, Good, Mediocre, Bad

Sunday

Program:	Program:	Program:	Program:
Reason:	Reason:	Reason:	Reason:
Rating:	Rating:	Rating:	Rating:
Instead of watching I decided to:	Instead of watching I decided to:	Instead of watching I decided to:	Instead of watching I decided to:

Monday

Program:	Program:	Program:	Program:
Reason:	Reason:	Reason:	Reason:
Rating:	Rating:	Rating:	Rating:
Instead of watching I decided to:	Instead of watching I decided to:	Instead of watching I decided to:	Instead of watching I decided to:

Tuesday

Program:	Program:	Program:	Program:
Reason:	Reason:	Reason:	Reason:
Rating:	Rating:	Rating:	Rating:
Instead of watching I decided to:	Instead of watching I decided to:	Instead of watching I decided to:	Instead of watching I decided to:

Wednesday

Program:	Program:	Program:	Program:
Reason:	Reason:	Reason:	Reason:
Rating:	Rating:	Rating:	Rating:
Instead of watching I decided to:	Instead of watching I decided to:	Instead of watching I decided to:	Instead of watching I decided to:

Thursday

Program:	Program:	Program:	Program:
Reason:	Reason:	Reason:	Reason:
Rating:	Rating:	Rating:	Rating:
Instead of watching I decided to:	Instead of watching I decided to:	Instead of watching I decided to:	Instead of watching I decided to:

Friday

Program:	Program:	Program:	Program:
Reason:	Reason:	Reason:	Reason:
Rating:	Rating:	Rating:	Rating:
Instead of watching I decided to:	Instead of watching I decided to:	Instead of watching I decided to:	Instead of watching I decided to:

Saturday

Program:	Program:	Program:	Program:
Reason:	Reason:	Reason:	Reason:
Rating:	Rating:	Rating:	Rating:
Instead of watching I decided to:	Instead of watching I decided to:	Instead of watching I decided to:	Instead of watching I decided to:

Watching critically will point up how many programs you regularly watch that don't measure up to your newfound standards of good programming. The following list is adapted from the Alliance for Children and Television for Health Canada.

Attributes of a Critical Viewer

1. A critical viewer can recognize when he or she is watching too much TV.
What to ask: Is watching TV causing me to neglect homework, chores, exercise, etc.? Has socializing become secondary to watching TV? Do I watch TV to avoid communicating with others?

2. A critical viewer can identify how conflict is resolved on the programs he or she watches, and decide to agree with the solution or find a better way to resolve the conflict.
What to ask: Was violence used to solve conflict? If so, was the person involved portrayed as a good guy? If a good guy performs violence, is that okay?

3. A critical viewer can recognize stereotypes being perpetuated on TV.
What to ask: Are women and children portrayed as helpless? Are senior citizens forgetful, inactive, or without any worth? What roles do blacks, Asians, others play? Are they shown in a slum, being bad guys, using bad language?

4. A critical viewer can identify what else is being sold besides the product on TV commercials.
What to ask: Do you think using that product will make you cool and attractive, like the actor or actress in the commercial? What are they not telling you about the product? Do you always believe it is a good product?

5. A critical viewer pays attention to the characteristics of the TV personality he or she identifies with.
What to ask: What is this TV character's occupation, family role, values? How does he or she dress, talk, behave? How is this character being treated by others?

6. A critical viewer questions the reliability or bias of information sources on TV, such as news or documentaries.
What to ask: Who is the authority conveying the information? Is there financial or political gain to be realized by presenting this point of view? What preconceived notions do you bring to the story?

WEEK THREE: START TO CUT BACK

Begin in little ways to cut back on TV time by using these simple rules. Keep only one TV active in the house. Cover any remaining sets or store them away in a closet.

1. Eliminate TV watching before school or during meals.

2. Choose three school nights on which TV cannot be watched.

3. Permit one hour of viewing on the remaining two school nights. If one hour is not enough, select an additional hour from PBS, the Discovery Channel, the Learning Channel, the History Channel, A & E, or another network that specializes in educational programming.

4. Determine, by family vote, how many viewing hours there should be on Saturday and Sunday.

5. On Sunday look at the TV section in the newspaper and choose as a family what you intend to watch each day of the coming week; then watch those shows together. Have each family member fill out, at the beginning of the week, the accompanying schedule.

Week Three TV Schedule

	Programs I Plan to Watch	No. of Hrs. I Plan to Watch	No. of Hrs. Actually Watched	No. of Hrs. + or − Today's Goal
Sun.				
Mon.				
Tues.				
Wed.				
Thurs.				
Fri.				
Sat.				
Totals				

* I made my week's goal.

+ I bettered my week's goal by _____ hour(s) and _____ minutes.

‡ I didn't make my goal, but I went over by only _____ hour(s) and _____ minutes.

While viewing television or videos during the week, take this advice from National Educational Television about good viewing habits:

Preparation is essential. Know as much as possible about a program before watching it. Talk about the show and give your children specific things to look for. This will make viewing active rather than only passive.

Sit at a direct angle and a good ten feet away from the set to ensure good vision. Being too close may be a health hazard.

Watch with your children, pointing out your thoughts as they occur. This makes the act of watching less solitary and more of a shared experience.

When the program is over, turn off the TV and turn to related activities: role-playing, dinner table conversation, books on the program's content, etc.

WEEK FOUR: THE BEGINNING OF LIFE WITHOUT TV

It's time to turn off the TV. Unplug all televisions, don't tease yourself by buying *TV Guide,* and if you are hooked on a soap, make sure you are out of the house when it is on. Make a game of this week. Hang signs around, saying: "This is an unplugged house." Post the following strategies on the refrigerator door and refer to them when you'd ordinarily turn on the TV.

- Call a friend and have a good chat.

- Compile a list of alternative activities and turn to any one of them instead of TV.

- Socialize more, have a potluck supper, invite your children's friends in.

- Keep a diary of your feelings.

Mud Pies and Mess: What to Expect in a TV-Free House

Your children will be happy to have a real family life again, and you will enjoy your new active, rather than passive, household. Most parents fear that their role with no TV will be one of magician, entertainer, and teacher all rolled into one. However, you will find yourself being no more than a catalyst. You'll be needed at first for suggestions, but soon the child in your children will return, and they will figure out exactly how to occupy themselves.

Few children will sit for more than a half hour twiddling their thumbs. They might turn to the refrigerator for a snack, call a friend, listen to music, but then they'll be off to discover things that were long forgotten. After all, it is in a child's nature to play, and so they will.

The rest of the family will catch on as well. Playing is as beneficial to adults as to children. When grown-ups stop playing, it is said, they tend to head for alternative escapes, such as alcohol, drugs, and lots of television. Instead of burying boredom and bad moods in front of the television you'll have time and reality to air feelings and thoughts about each person's day. Helping each other deal with frustrations actively rather than passively in front of a TV screen is the path to vital living.

To equip your house to function without TV, you'll need to fill in some of the blank spaces where the TV used to be with equally addictive and attractive forms of entertainment.

Create a Play Space

Need space? Be prepared to relinquish the dining room, a section of the family room, the basement, or any other area of your house or apartment that is attractive to and available for children. Children need a private place that is theirs alone to carry out their experiments, games, and other secret activities free from the scrutiny of parents. Even if the spot is under a stairwell or in the corner of a busy room, your children will know it's theirs. Parents, resign yourself to the fact that in these special play spaces anything goes—within reason. Children's corners will never be *Better Homes and Gardens* perfect.

Stock a Sports Center

A household sports center or dugout area is an important feature in a televisionless house. It can be a large, empty closet, a series of boxes along the garage wall, or a specifically built open-cupboard area. The sports center should be filled with all kinds of equipment—gloves, bats, tees, jump ropes, tennis balls, basketballs, air pumps, and chalk with which to make obstacle courses, baselines, and hopscotch paths. Be willing to resupply lost balls and other equipment.

Supply a Craft Table

A dining-room table works best for a variety of crafts. Cover it with newspaper and a sheet of plastic. Along the wall build a simple bookcase area. Buy various-size baskets into which you can put crayons, beeswax, clay, glue, paint, brushes, scissors, pencils, Magic Markers, and other materials. Have paper, model kits, activity books, paper dolls, and anything else you can think of sitting in full view of your children. You will be amazed at how often your children will gravitate to this craft area throughout the day. A craft table is infinitely more inviting than a television screen.

During week four designate one or two nights for family games and projects. A family night is great for holiday projects, crafts, long games of Monopoly, or card games. Here are other family strategies and suggestions for getting through week four:

- Resurrect the family radios and use them for news.

- Plan to do some major overhaul on the house, such as cleaning the basement, painting the living room, or washing the windows.

- Plan different menus and try new recipes. Buy a cookbook for your children so they can enjoy the art of baking. Pop popcorn. It's irresistible.

- If you have a regular sporting activity, such as tennis, paddleball, squash, or handball, arrange for additional court time, especially during what were previously your prime TV viewing hours.

- Fix the broken bike or some other item that has been waiting to be fixed.

- Plan a garage sale featuring all the useless items you bought because of television commercials.

- Get out of the house. Go to the movies, take a walk, go out to dinner.

- Renew old hobbies. Did you have a stamp collection when you were young?

- Invite another family over for dinner, potluck-style, once a week.

- Read your children to sleep. If they're too old for this, try reading a good short story out loud to the whole family.

- Plan a family night at the library.

- Sort your slides, and start organizing all your family pictures.

- Go Rollerblading, bicycling, roller skating.

- Find out about community center and park activities.

- Plan a picnic.

- Organize a block party.

- Plant a garden.

- Join a choir.

- Camp out in the backyard.

- Paint a mural in a room, basement, or garage.

- Go dancing—take dance lessons.

Bad-Day Survival Techniques

In every family there will be days of boredom, rain, sickness, and disappointment, or days when parents are especially busy and can't spend too much time with their children. These are the times when television used to come in handy. Here are some suggestions for surprises that can help you through these days.

The comfort bag. Keep a shopping bag filled with manila envelopes that have in them such things as forgotten toys, old pocketbooks filled with junk (supermarket coupons, play money, old keys), stickers and Scotch tape, playing cards, scissors, costume jewelry, a magnifying glass, Magic Markers, beeswax, small dolls, a magic slate, paper dolls, marbles, and a harmonica. Let your sad, attention-seeking child pick an envelope or two and work out a good afternoon of play.

The reserved kitchen drawer. Stock a kitchen drawer with junk such as a few old kitchen tools and other objects. The selection of objects depends on the age of the child, of course, but this should work for children from eighteen months through kindergarten. Throw in little toys and amusements left behind in case you need them, especially on days when you're stuck in the kitchen.

The surprise box.   Have a box hidden away into which you put toys picked up on sale, coloring and activity books, crayons, packs of baseball cards, miniatures for dollhouses, yo-yos, and other items to perk up and keep a child busy. The surprise box shouldn't be overworked, or it will become a bribe. Keep it as an emergency measure. The surprise box can be adapted for all ages.

6

Keeping It Going with Equal-Time Activities

〜〜〜〜〜

Y ou have arrived. You went through an entire week with no television. Sure, it took a few tough weeks to accomplish this, but don't look back now. Instead, proceed. You've worked up a momentum that will carry you through to establishing a selective, intelligent viewing program and maintaining it permanently.

Of course, you will have doubts. One day it will rain or snow, and everyone will be out of ideas for things to do. This is the time when the children used to head for the television set. Turn to the list you have posted and remember the "Six Reasons Why Your Children Need to Break the TV Habit."

WHAT TO EXPECT WHEN YOUR HOME IS TV-FREE

Excising excessive television watching from your life will lead to other consequences. Here's what you should expect:

Expect a higher noise level. On weekend mornings you'll probably hear balls bouncing, water swishing, doors slamming, and music playing. The consolation prize is that the new sounds are friendlier and more pleasant than the deadening beat of cartoons.

Expect a messier house. Young children busy at play make messes, which, of course, they can learn to clean up. They like to play near their parents when they are inside, which means a messy kitchen and family room. They enjoy bringing worms, caterpillars, and lost treasures to the kitchen door to show them off. This means dirt tracked inside, but it's all in the name of good, healthy play!

66 *Television, in the main, is being used to distract, delude, amuse, and insulate us.* **99**

—Edward R. Murrow

Expect a more active household. Children who are not tucked away in front of a TV screen are running in and out, jumping off ledges, hopping, climbing, and, with all this, falling, bleeding, and crying. Generally they are involved, very happy, and very tired at the end of the day.

Expect more demands. Children will want to go to the library or the bookstore. They'll ask to be chauffeured to friends' houses, and they'll want to have friends over to sleep. They will start huge collections of rocks, animals, coins, or stamps—all of which will mean you'll have to supply some time, money, and patience.

Expect to spend money. You'll find yourself buying sports

equipment and craft projects, and paying for some library fines as well as tickets for movies and for excursions to bowling alleys and skating rinks. Older children, however, can start earning the money for their new hobbies by doing special chores—walking the dog, cleaning the cat box, raking the leaves, working for neighbors.

Expect the return of some of your favorite things. This includes calm children, spouses not in front of the television all weekend, family discussions, lingering at the dinner table, time for problem-solving and resolving conflicts, discussion of upcoming activities, and fun.

Expect permanent changes in your children. Unlike lung damage from too much cigarette smoking or liver disease from too much drinking, the damages incurred from too much television are repairable. Many of the symptoms of TV abuse will simply disappear with the disappearance of TV viewing.

Take the demand for toys and foods advertised on television, for example. Less-TV parents boast of a certain smugness that comes while holiday and birthday shopping. "The demands from the children are less," they report. "There I stand being creative in the toy store, of all places. I go up and down the aisles looking for surprises, things my kids don't even know exist because they don't see commercials anymore."

Being responsible for their own entertainment also slows down children and makes them more patient. They no longer have to have what they want *right now!* Parties, creative play, and sporting skills all lead to organized thought. No longer is everything instant, like the flick of the TV button, and as time goes on, children without television develop a respect for process, for things that take time.

Mothers rarely report hearing "I'm bored" when the television is gone. Many children's interests move on to musical instruments, hands-on projects, and organized sports. These activities leave little time to be bored.

Good conversation regenerates in televisionless homes. There is now time to really listen to one another around the dinner table and into the evening hours. Children regain some of their powers of focus and concentration. Those who were previously inarticulate and inattentive have a chance to practice talking and listening again. Gradually their thought patterns and sentence structure lose the jagged, hesitant flavor of TV talk, and language becomes smoother and less painful. Nightmares are often replaced with pleasant dreams as storytelling becomes part of the bedtime ritual.

Not only are negative aspects of TV eliminated once a family has decided on less television, but also there are now more important, positive goals that can be achieved. The most worthy of these, perhaps, is providing situations and an environment for family members, especially children, to develop into whole people. A whole person is mentally, physically, spiritually, and emotionally alive. If a person, adult or child, has given over a large portion of his or her time to television, it becomes impossible for him to develop fully. By participating in activities that will develop each aspect of the personality, you are stimulating one part or another of yourself and thus growing no matter what your age.

WORKING OUT A FAMILY PROGRAM

A healthy amount of television is ten hours per week. According to Dr. Kenneth Hopkins' study for the National Institute of Education, ten hours of TV a week may actually enhance a student's achievement in school slightly. Over and above ten hours, the student's achievement level diminishes, as well as his or her reading ability.

Continue with the TV rules you established in week three.

Note particularly:

Rule 1. No television before school, during meals, after school, or before homework is done.

Rule 2. No televisions in the bedrooms. If possible, keep only one set active, and put it in the least-inviting room of the house. Research shows that people gravitate less to the television when it's not in a main room.

Rule 3. No television on several designated nights during the week. Better yet, don't allow any regular TV viewing during the week.

Rule 4. For every half hour of television watching, one hour must be devoted to physical exercise, reading, or playing.

Rule 5. Use the stereo or radio if you need background sound.

Rule 6. Don't turn on the television at random. Watch only those programs that have been selected for the week's viewing.

Rule 7. Don't buy or read TV-related magazines.

These rules have been designed to eliminate 85 percent of all television now being watched in most households. You will find that they easily become the basis for your new way of life.

For the first four to six weeks after you've completed the Four-Week No-TV Program, family members should get together on Sunday evening to review the television schedule in the newspaper and plan the week's viewing. After doing this for several weeks, it probably won't be necessary to fill out the charts. In fact, you may find yourself leaving notes to remind you to watch something special.

IDEAS AND INSTRUCTIONS FOR BABY-SITTERS

Remember to tell baby-sitters about the no-television regimen so that house rules aren't violated as soon as you go out. Give your sitter a schedule of activities with definite times so there's a real program to follow. For instance, if the sitter is scheduled to arrive at six and the children have already eaten dinner, there is time for a game from six to six-thirty, stories from six-thirty to seven, a bath and getting ready for bed from seven to seven-thirty, and a bedtime snack at about eight.

Many young children hate to see their parents go out for the evening, but the blow is softened if they have a sitter who makes the occasions special. Let the sitter prepare simple snacks such as popcorn, milkshakes, or ice cream cones. If the sitter is coming during the day, leave a list of games selected from lists provided.

Finally, if you are down to one portable television set, keep it in the closet when a baby-sitter is scheduled to come. Out of sight, out of mind. You can tell the sitter where to find it if she wants to watch after the children are asleep.

IDEAS FOR WORKING PARENTS

If working parents have followed the Four-Week No-TV Program and established television awareness in the home, then TV should cease to be a major problem after school and in the evenings.

"We're talking about a relatively short period of time," said Jane Sherman, the mother of four children under thirteen, in an interview with the author. "Three to five is when most children of working mothers are home alone. Snacks, activities, chores, and homework eat up those two hours in no time. Television is simply not a necessity." To help remind her children of this, Jane has placed a sign on the TV screen that said: "No TV, please." What do the children do? The Shermans live in a New York City apartment and belong to a nearby gym so that the children can play indoors during the winter. In better weather there is an organized playground near their home. "My kids are also into music," she continues. "If they don't have a lesson, in all likelihood they are home drumming up music on their own. We have purchased some recording equipment, amplifiers, and a keyboard so they can make music together."

The key is having confidence in your children and having them honor your need for them to be physically and emotionally safe. "I don't want my children closeted in the house and yet I want them safe," explained one suburban mom. "They are permitted to play anywhere on our property. Also, my husband is great. We have two boys, and when he gets home in the late afternoon and they are outside he never refuses them a game of catch or pitching baseballs to them."

Most working parents who are succeeding in keeping their kids off television have designed an after-school schedule with their children that includes chores, possible activities, and homework, and also lay down rules on where they can and cannot play. For many, specific projects on the computer for children of appropriate ages are used as entertainment after school.

Residents of one cul-de-sac in suburban New Jersey where virtually every house has both parents working pooled their resources and hired a high school boy and girl to greet the children as they get off the bus, make a healthy snack in a different house each day, and organize outside activities until the parents get home. Since the street is a dead end, the kids are free to skateboard, Rollerblade, and cycle.

Still, the greatest problem for working and single parents is fighting off exhaustion. "I want to be there for my kids when I get home," said one mom, "but there are always so many other things pulling at me; dinner, laundry, my husband. The main thing we do is sit down to dinner together and everyone has to take their turn at sharing something about their day. One night a week we go out for something simple, and with no phone ringing and neighborhood kids dropping by, we actually get some special sharing time."

One teacher in Boston, also a single mom, does her homework (grading papers and such) along with her two daughters at the dining-room table. In that way they get to spend time together, she can offer help if needed, and they can share an additional hour before dinner. "It's much better than each of us retreating to our separate rooms. I always rummage through their backpacks looking for notes, school programs, and such, which become part of our conversations. Now that they are nine and twelve they do household chores after school, for which I pay them."

Another working mom, in suburban New York, has formed a baby-sitting co-op with neighbors. Each mother negotiated for a four-day workweek with her employer, and each has a separate day off. On that day the neighborhood children come to that mother's house after school. These same women barter for other services. "It's like we have an extended family," said one. "Not only do we help each other, but we also share problems and issues. Because we all want to keep TV at a minimum, the kids know it and hardly ever ask to see a show." While this arrangement is clearly not possible for all families, it demonstrates that where there's a will, there's a way.

A mother of two who is an executive with an insurance firm takes one day off per month to take her children to the museum, the zoo, the circus—something special. The same mother staggers her children's bedtimes so each child receives some focused attention.

"My kids know that if they do their homework before I get home we will do something together in the evening; perhaps play a game. This isn't every night, because we're all too tired, but we try for togetherness twice a week."

The consensus among working parents who are trying to balance their children's lives and keep TV at a minimum is to keep a sense of humor and not beat up on themselves when they find that they and the children are backsliding toward television. "I'm always willing to replenish their craft table, buy them arts and crafts, and yes, suggest watching television together when none of us has the energy to be active or interactive. But I must say it is the last resort, like dessert after a big meal."

Action for Children's Television (ACT) has devised a rather clever game called Switch. Teach your children the five switches ACT recommends:

Switch from buying a toy to making one. In one hour of children's television it is possible to see more than ten commercials for toys. These toys are often expensive—fifteen to twenty dollars apiece, more than most families can afford to spend. Instead of buying a toy, it's fun to make a puppet, plant a seed, string some spools, or design a city out of cartons.

Switch to an apple, an orange, or a carrot. Ninety-eight percent of U.S. children suffer from tooth decay. The substance most likely to cause cavities is sugar. With few exceptions the only foods advertised on children's television are candies, cookies, sugared cereals, drink sweeteners, and soft drinks. Stop buying those products, and dream up your own super snacks, such as popcorn, cheese fingers, nuts, orange slices, and apple wedges.

Switch to public television. There is no advertising on public television, but much children's programming, as well as good dramas, concerts, documentaries, and science programs for older children.

Switch off the TV and take a walk, read a book, visit a zoo, go to a museum, play with a friend.

Switch to doing something about children's television. Talk about television to your friends and analyze why commercials are effective so you can see how to weaken their power over the family.

ACTIVITIES FOR PRESCHOOLERS

The hardest children to entertain are often preschoolers, because they are home all day. Here are several easy activities that will keep toddlers through six-year-olds busy, if a little noisy! (Asterisks indicate activities that are explained in detail.)

dolls*

playing house

simple puzzles

rhythm band*

coloring, painting, drawing

simple crafts

leaf piles*

hide-and-seek

Simon says

snow play

records

hike in the house*

play group*

dress up*

water and bath tub play*

dough play*

ball games

Feely-Bag stories*

slime*

bean bags

block bowling*

box houses*

paper punching bags*

masking tape roads*

tumbling mattress

cards*

- *Dolls.* Keep a bagful of colorful and silky fabric, rickrack, ribbon, and other trim and old scarves from which your children can create doll clothes. Capes and skirts can be made without sewing.

- *Rhythm band.* Preschoolers love cymbals, triangles, drums, and tambourines. Harmonicas and kazoos are fun, too. For homemade instruments try the following:

  1. Fill soda bottles to different levels with water. Tap with a spoon for various tones, or blow over the top of the bottles.

  2. Take a shoe box and string it with rubber bands to make a harp.

3. Fill an empty plastic bottle with a quarter cup of rice. Cover and shake.

4. Use an empty oatmeal box as a drum.

- *Leaf piles.* Raking and piling leaves can be fun for everyone. If your children have their own rakes, let them loose to create a leaf fort or a leaf path. For a real treat let children heap the leaves high and trek through the pile. It's also fun for children to jump into leaf piles and bury themselves.

- *Hike in the house.* This is good when other children visit. Have picnic lunches packed for everyone. Children go for a hike through the house pretending that the stairs are "up the mountain." "Past the forest" is through the dining room chairs; "through the city" could be the living room. Finally, arrive at a spot for the picnic. Be sure to clean up the campsite before returning home.

- *Play group.* Join with other parents and set up a three- or four-child group, rotating houses. For advice see *The Playgroup Handbook* by Laura P. Broad (New York: St. Martin's Press, 1991).

- *Dress up.* Keep a boxful of cast-off ties, slips, hats, purses, costume jewelry, scarves, and other accessories. Children can play endlessly, dressing up as a favorite character or making up costumes.

- *Water and bathtub play.* Save laundry sprinkles, plastic bottles with squeeze tops, funnels, measuring spoons, sponges, plastic cups, cars, boats, and suction basters for this soothing experience. Water play in the kitchen sink, bathtub, or wading pool is the best for preschoolers. When they are out, let them explore puddles, ponds, streams, and of course, the ocean. Bathtime is one of the highlights of daily rhythm. Water play is reminiscent of his or her prenatal security.

- *Dough play.* This is a must recipe for mothers of all preschool children. Mix two teaspoons of cream of tartar, a cup of flour, a half cup of salt, a tablespoon of oil, and a cup of water to make a smooth paste. Cook slowly in a saucepan until the dough forms a ball. Knead for a few minutes after it has cooled down, and store in a fridge in an airtight container. Then use cookie cutters, rolling pins, or plastic utensils to create objects.

- *Feely-Bag stories.* If you want to tell spontaneous stories but are stuck for ideas, try using a Feely-Bag. Make a drawstring bag out of fabric remnant and keep in it a collection of mystery objects such as wooden ornaments, marbles, toys, dolls, and pinecones. At storytime give your child the bag and let her feel the objects without opening the bag. Then let her pick one out without looking and begin a story based on the object. Stop from time to time so she can add to the script.

- *Slime.* Mix two cups of water and a little food coloring with six cups of cornflower/cornstarch to create a nice, thick slime. If possible, arrange this activity outside on a plastic-covered surface. Dress the child in a plastic apron and let him plunge his hands and arms into the slime to make patterns with it. Slime is also a good potion for those children into playing fairy tale.

- *Block bowling.* Set up cardboard boxes at one end of the kitchen floor, and let children roll a rubber ball toward them to see how many boxes they can knock down. A good rainy-day sport.

- *Box houses.* Rescue large-appliance boxes whenever you see them on the street after delivery of a washing machine or dryer. They are perfect for making houses and forts, and children love to have their own private place in the house. Use poster paints for windows and trim.

- *Paper punching bags.* Stuff paper bags or plastic bags with crumbled newspapers. Hang bags from the ceiling, and let children punch them apart until they get tired of this activity.

- *Masking tape roads.* Permit children to design a road around the house; mark out the road with masking tape. Children can run cars over their roads.

- *Cards.* Even a young child can play solitaire by putting together all the red cards or all the cards with matching numbers. Kindergartners can arrange the cards in ace–ten sequence. Don't underestimate the entertainment value of a deck of cards.

ACTIVITIES FOR ELEMENTARY SCHOOL–AGE CHILDREN

Six- to ten-year-olds often have scheduled after-school activities, and some may have homework or instrument practice. Here's a list to supplement the regular round of activities:

reading	board games
tinfoil baseball*	jump rope
Nerf football	acorn fights
basement bowling	hopscotch
ball games	weekly library visits
darts	crafts*
newspaper war	flashlight tag*
holiday crafts	skateboarding
meal preparation*	roller-skating
woodworking*	tag
pen pal program	collection/hobby
bike riding	kite flying
baseball card flip	jacks
solitaire	pet care

- *Tinfoil baseball.* This is a helpful game when real baseball can't be played. Crumple up tinfoil to make a small ball, and bat it with a stick. No harm done, lots of fun, and nothing gets broken.

- *Meal preparation.* At this age a child can be very helpful around dinnertime setting the table, peeling carrots, breaking up salad. This is also a good way to spend some time with the parent who is making the meal.

- *Woodworking.* Hammers, nails, blocks of wood, sandpaper, vices, screws, and screwdrivers will keep any child happy for a good length of time. Suggest that your child make wooden sculptures or model houses or just practice hammering.

- *Crafts.* Wooden wine crates and grape boxes make marvelous dollhouses and forts for soldiers. Likewise, orange crates make nice bedside tables. If you are the start-from-scratch type, visit your local lumberyard and pick up supplies for building bookcases or shelves.

- *Flashlight tag.* A good substitute for a favorite prime-time TV program is flashlight tag. It is played outside at night. The person who is "it" has a flashlight; when he shines the light on someone, that person is caught.

ACTIVITIES FOR JUNIOR HIGH SCHOOLERS

At this age children often have a busy schedule, and it's easy to overlook family activities and hobbies that can lay the foundation for a lifelong interest.

reading	jogging
model building	after-school Y program
ongoing games*	getting in shape

challenging puzzles*   chores
journal   clubs
moviegoing   earning pocket money*
stamp or coin collecting   voluteer activites*
team sports

- *Ongoing games.* Set aside time after dinner a few nights a week to play time-consuming games such as Monopoly. You can continue the same game nightly for a week if need be. You'll be practically bankrupt on Tuesday and recover your losses on Thursday! Various word and card games, chess, and checkers also can be played on this basis. Keep a weekly score.

- *Challenging puzzles.* Here's a lost treat. A started puzzle on a card table is an enticing activity for a long winter evening. Leave the puzzle out until it's finished. Anyone can drop by at any time to fit in a piece.

- *Earning pocket money.* At this age children can start earning pocket money by doing chores in the neighborhood—walking dogs, raking leaves, baby-sitting. If you want your children to do some extra chores around the house beyond their regular assignments, you might consider paying them a small wage to rake leaves, help clean up the backyard, and so on.

- *Volunteer activities.* As children approach their teens, they can investigate some of the volunteer activities in the neighborhood at hospitals and senior citizen centers and through church and school-organized groups. Organize community cleanup.

These suggestions are meant to get you started in alternate activities. They are only a small sample of the possibilities your children will enjoy. You'll surely discover many more.

SPECIAL EVENTS

So now you've developed a houseful of television conscious-ness with a program to back it up, and suddenly you're faced with those once-in-a-lifetime specials that television brings right into your living room. I'm talking about events such as the Olympic Games, presidential conventions, the World Series, the Super Bowl, and made-for-television documentaries or miniseries. There's no doubt that television is at its best when it is live; live coverage of special events is one of the true benefits of television. Therefore it's surely advisable to make some exceptions for specials and major news events such as an inauguration or a shuttle launch.

Here are a few suggestions for keeping abreast of special events without becoming totally glued to the television set and seduced back into heavy television viewing.

The Olympics

Watch the opening and closing ceremonies if they interest you and the summaries of daily events. In addition, choose specif-ic events to watch, just as if you were buying tickets for them. Take in events such as track and field that your children can go out and try on their own, or tune into an unusual sport to intro-duce the family to it. Try to avoid so-called background pieces that are designed to keep you watching the entire spectrum of Olympics coverage, even when nothing is happening. This approach will work for other events that continue from one day to the next.

The World Series

The temptation is to watch the World Series on television. Actually, radio coverage has always been more descriptive and enthusiastic. Listen to the games for the most part, and plan to watch only the last game or two. Try to squeeze this and other sports coverage into your weekly ten-hour allotment.

Presidential Conventions

Save your energy and television viewing time for the third night of the conventions, when there are actual debate over the platform and actual balloting for the candidates. And, of course, watch the acceptance speech. Children can benefit from watching the conventions, but don't overdo it. Try to steer clear of padded background coverage.

The Super Bowl

What can you say about the Super Bowl, one of the biggest TV events of the year? The hype is often greater than the game. Nevertheless, almost everyone will want to watch, so have some friends over, and make it a social occasion. For a little penance, cut down on your viewing during the rest of the week so you can fit the Super Bowl into your normal television allotment. Try the same approach with other major sports events.

Documentary Dramas and Miniseries

It's quite a commitment to follow a program that runs five nights in a row. However, if one of these programs seems worthwhile to a member of the family, watch the first night, catch a summary before the next night's episode, and tune in to the final installment. For my part, I usually find a good book on the subject as informative as the television treatment. A long series, such as those featured on PBS, or a special documentary or report can easily be worked into the week's schedule as part of your regular viewing. If the series or special is scheduled for one of your no-TV nights, adjust your schedules for those weeks.

News Events

A presidential news conference or major speech is valuable for older children and can be easily fitted into the week's viewing schedule. The same would hold true for space shots, major news events, and spectacles such as royal weddings or state occasions. Include these events in your week's schedule when you know about them in advance. If they're unexpected but significant, adjust your viewing plan for the week, watch the events as a family, and follow up with magazine and newspaper details.

HOLIDAYS

A friend of mine and her husband traveled from New York to Indiana last Thanksgiving to visit her parents. The trip was expensive, and it meant taking a few vacation days from their jobs. Thus it was both disappointing and exasperating to them that the television set was on during their entire visit. "Even when friends dropped by to see us, the set stayed on," my friend recalled. "It seemed that television was more important to my parents than I was."

In many homes holiday traditions have become television specials instead of family gatherings. When suburban New York children were told that they would participate in a no-TV week during December, they booed because they didn't want to miss the television specials.

Here are a few suggestions to keep television under control during the holidays.

Thanksgiving

This is a day for the whole family to be together. Save the football games for Saturday. Spend the early part of Thursday preparing the meal and readying the house, assigning jobs to each child. This is easier said than done if adult men are coming. How can you handle this situation? Stash the television in a closet, or cover it with a tablecloth and nut bowls so no one can gather around it as the day progresses.

Holidays

Choose only the very best holiday specials, and don't watch more than one a week. Instead of TV specials substitute "family specials" such as holiday crafts, baking, and reading classic stories (perhaps a long one over several nights). Invite other families to join in, or have them over for a brunch, a luncheon, or an Advent gathering, during which the entire family can make ornaments, sing carols, wrap gifts, and do other things to prepare for the big day.

New Year's Day

There is a Scottish tradition that on New Year's Eve and New Year's Day friends and relatives drop in on one another. Freed from television, start off the New Year with some visits or throw a big open house. Use the covered television as a place for hors d'oeuvres.

ADULT VIEWING PROBLEMS, OR IF YOU TALK THE TALK, WALK THE WALK

The goal is to cut back your children's TV watching to no more than two hours a day, as the National PTA, the National Association for the Education of Young People, and the American Academy of Pediatrics suggest. As parents we also need to alter our viewing habits if we are to succeed.

One of the many problems families encounter when they try to cut down on television is that parents, not children, may be the serious viewers. So often the children would just as soon have the television set off and their parents available to them instead, but some parents have a heavy TV habit to break. As you work to control your family's television intake, remember these points:

You are your child's primary model. If you watch more than fifteen hours of TV a week you are probably providing a model of unconscious, passive viewing for a good portion of that time.

You don't want to be a hypocrite. If you require your children to cut back on their TV viewing, but they see you watching, they can rightfully question the fairness of your edict. They'll learn that it's okay for parents to say one thing and do another. Instead of moving forward with a joint effort to regulate TV in your home, your efforts could backfire and lead to more conflict around TV viewing.

Your time is their time. This may be the most important point of all. The less time you spend watching *Roseanne* or *Monday Night Football,* the

66 Children who are protected from television and who are involved in meaningful, creative, and physical activities can practice to the full their sensory experience, physical alertness, and skills in order to grow thoroughly accustomed to their body and its possibilities. 99

—Michaela Glöekler, as written in John Thomson, *Natural Childhood*

more time you have for your children and the more time you have to share activities with them. These hours are the real prime time where you can serve as an educator for your child. These are the hours your child will remember the most when growing up: the times you showed them how to make a bird feeder, or took them to the museum, or coached the soccer team. Go for it!

Sports Freaks, News Nuts, and Soap Opera Addicts

Of course, even for adults, there are special problems to overcome. Here are some suggestions for some of the more difficult television habits to break:

Sports Freaks

There once was an eight-year-old boy named Henry. He hated football, or so he said to his mother. One bright fall day his mother happened to gaze out the window, and there was Henry, playing football with his father. After the game she remarked, "I thought you told me that you hated football, Henry." "Oh," said the boy with a grin, "I hate to watch football, but I love to play it."

After hearing this story, many fathers make a conscious effort to play a bit more with their children rather than leaving all the sports action to the television.

Television sports has changed marriage, family life, and major holidays. Thanksgiving dinner is arranged so it doesn't coincide with a football game; Easter dinner is usually interrupted by the Masters Golf Tournament. Television sports have taken active fathers and made them into passive spectators. The advent of cable and sports channels has only increased the possibilities for watching instead of participating. Many of us can relate to this. In my family we watch no more that one hour of TV a day—except sports!

Here are some tips for controlling sports viewing:

- Treat television sports the same way you treat a live sports event for which you buy tickets. If you buy tickets to a soccer, baseball, or basketball game, you plan to give your full attention to that one event. Choose to watch one major event when you sit down to watch sports, not an entire day of televised events.

- For every sporting event you watch on television, play one game of your favorite sport.

- To repay family time spent watching a sports event, participate with family members in a casual game of catch, football, Frisbee, etc.

- Remind yourself that activity, not passivity, lengthens life and keeps the cardiovascular system healthy. Cardiologists believe that, in part, passive television viewing accounts for the sharp increase in heart disease among younger men.

News Nuts

In defense of their television habit, people frequently tell me, "I only watch the news." My answer is in the form of a question: "How much news?"

The news shows on television are fast becoming the medium's most popular form of entertainment. In many areas a viewer can watch twenty-four hours of news programming on CNN, CNBC, C-Span, and Headline News. Add to these staggering viewership totals for magazine-type programs such as *20/20, 60 Minutes,* and *Dateline,* and the viewer can accumulate not only large doses of daily news but also become well informed on every conceivable background or feature story.

I talked with a former news addict—a history teacher who justified his habit because of the subject he taught. "I thought I needed to watch the news every evening to stay informed, until I realized all that watching was giving me less and less real information. I quit the news and television altogether some ten years ago in favor of reading books, some newspapers, getting a master's degree, and just turning my interests in other directions. My life has changed dramaticallly for the better."

But are you really being fully informed by watching those

endless rounds of news shows? Don Bresnahan, a producer of television news documentaries, explains television news this way: "To the vast majority of news-hungry Americans . . . TV news offers all the news they want, all the news they think they need. This, perhaps, is the greatest sin of TV news; it has conditioned people to believe that what we have shown and told them is THE NEWS. It isn't, and everyone writing, reporting, editing, directing, producing, and anchoring knows it isn't. We are in the headline business. We are in the tip-of-the-iceberg business. We pretend, in our own defense, that we are only whetting your appetite, and firmly insist that when you have finished viewing one of your local or network newscasts, you should rush out and buy a printed source for the rest of the story. We are guilty of giving you too little because we are desperately afraid that you really don't want any more."

With this in mind it may be easier to break the news addiction, especially for people who want time for family talk at dinner and in the early evening. The family will surely benefit more from discussion of a news event than from a television broadcast. Try these simple rules:

1. View at most a half hour of television news a day. Test a few programs until you find the one that serves you best, and watch just that one.

2. If you feel you must watch the national news at six-thirty, do so with a small portable, away from young children. If your children are in the upper elementary grades, watch with them, ready to explain stories that may seem confusing or frightening.

3. Replace morning television news with radio news.

4. Subscribe to one good comprehensive newspaper and read it thoroughly. You will not only get a broader picture of the story but sometimes several points of view.

5. So you don't feel out of touch with world events and trends, during the weaning process watch PBS's *Washington Week in Review.*

6. If you must watch more than one news show a day, choose a second show after the children are in bed.

Understanding the News

Even though the news seems significant—something we really *must* watch to stay informed—the programs are developed no differently than entertainment programs. And just as all television programming is in the business of attracting your attention to sell you something, the news is no different. To help your children understand that the news is no more sacred than anything else on television, here are some tips to help you.

Put on a live family news show. Do the following:

1. Decide on the number of new stories.

2. Assign reporters, an anchor, a writer, and an editor.

3. If you can, videotape your newscast to show friends and relatives.

4. Involve the neighborhood to create a neighborhood news show.

Help them to understand the whole picture. Although the news is based on reality, it's only a small part of reality. For most of us, life does not imitate the images of a newscast.

Talk back to the TV. As with any other type of programming, if children hear what you think, it will help them to process the images they are seeing and hearing. Let them know if you don't think that a story has been fairly reported or leaves anything important out.

Positive responses are important. If you're pleased with the treatment an important issue receives, let them hear it.

Talk to your kids. The news can be a springboard for discussion. Again, as with any television show, we can use what we see in the news to talk about difficult issues such as racism, war, death, AIDS, social issues, or sexuality. You know your children best and know which questions they will respond to.

Read between the lines. Ask critical questions. Are we getting the whole story? What stories are not being covered? What are the sources for a story? Is information missing that might help you to understand the story? If there is a story that your child is particularly interested in or frightened of, find out more about it. You may know someone who is involved in or has been affected by something that concerns or interests your child.

Plan a trip. Visit the neighborhood fire or police station, or arrange a visit to a factory, farm, sports facility, or television newsroom. If you are lucky enough to live near a library, zoo, or museum, there are many wonderful things to see and talk about. These trips will bring your kids in touch with reality, up close and personal real stuff, not just the outrageous.

Soap Opera Addicts

Perhaps the hardest habit to control is watching television soap operas. The story line is written to entice the addicted viewer to tune in tomorrow and tomorrow and tomorrow. The characters on the soaps are particularly entertaining, and many find it both fun and stimulating to live vicariously through their favorite stars as an escape from domestic drudgery.

However, there are some real drawbacks to soap opera addiction:

1. The shows are on when children are up and around, and the sexual explicitness as well as the tragic story lines can be upsetting to small children. Once I was a *Search for Tomorrow* addict. Years later my children asked what happened to one of the young characters who had lost his parents and had no real home life.

2. Being stuck on a soap or several soaps means daily watching. Children learn by example, and mothers aren't setting a very good one by avoiding other activities so they can watch *their* programs. Many women won't take their children to the park during soap time. They take the receiver off the hook and refuse to schedule activities that interfere with the soap schedule.

3. Many lonely housewives feel let down directly after watching their daily soap opera. The compulsive need to see the show is never satisfied by the show itself. This feeling will affect your children. They will also believe that TV characters are real and meaningful.

Breaking away from soap operas is not easy, but success stories abound. Here are some pointers:

1. Begin easing away from your favorite show by watching only Monday and Friday. You will get all the story line information you need during those two days.

2. Supplement the story line, if needed, by reading the weekly plot in the newspaper.

3. Plan to be out of the house while your soap is on the air. Plan a scheduled activity such as a tennis game or a hairdresser appointment so you must attend.

4. If you need the escapism that soap operas provide, read a good novel.

5. Set a time limit after which you will cut out seeing the Monday segment for your soap; two weeks after, cut out Friday.

Note the following from Vartan Gregorian, former president of Brown University, as reported in the October 1996 issue of *Family Weekly:* "Consider making TV a chore rather than an amusement. Let children watch four hours a day if they want to, but require them to write papers on what they see. My objection to television is not only the time it wastes but also the passivity it brings. It produces isolation, not communication. If children had to critique what they watched, it might even serve to reduce violence on the screen."

More Help for the Unplugged Home

*T*here's more than one way to trim the television habit. If your consciousness has been raised about your family video habits, yet you still feel your family indulges too much, the following list of pointers will help you trim hours off of watching in your home, even if you are not able to put the full four-week program into effect.

QUICK TIPS FOR GETTING UNPLUGGED

Using some or all of these tips will have a dramatic effect on life in your home.

Avoid using television and video games as a baby-sitter. It might be convenient for busy parents, but it can set a dangerous precedent. Instead of always using media for entertainment or diversion, try planning some other fun activity for the whole family.

Limit the use of television and video games. Keep it to no more than one or two quality hours per day. Set situation limits, too. No TV or video games before school, during the day, during meals, or before homework is finished.

Be aware of the messages being sent to your child. Remember, the younger the child, the more impressionable he or she is. You should know what values and information are being communicated directly to your kid's brain through television, computers, and video games.

Keep TV out of your child's bedroom. This will cut down the viewing time and keep your child from watching when you are not around.

Turn the TV off during mealtimes. Use the time to catch up and connect with one another. Talk over the day and begin generating good conversation.

Turn the set on only when you decide there's something worth watching. Don't turn it on to "see if there's something on." Don't channel-surf. Parents are often as guilty of this as their children are.

Don't make the TV set the focal point of the house. Families watch less TV and play fewer video games if the sets are not located in the center of their lives.

Watch what your kids are watching. That's the best way to find out what they're viewing. And you can discuss it with them while the show is in progress.

Be careful of what your kids see right before bedtime. Emotion-invoking images may linger and intrude into sleep.

Learn about the movies that are playing and the videos and games that are popular and available. Make sure your kids know what your rules are for appropriate viewing and listening. Review all choices in advance.

Become media-literate. Acquire critical viewing skills your-self, and teach them to your kids. Understand how and why media do what they do. Learn about advertising and its pur-poses and methods.

Limit your own TV viewing. If you're always glued to the TV, your kids will be, too. Don't let your kids observe material from "your" program. Set a good example by moderating your own use of media. Do something active with your time instead.

Let your voice be heard. Let program decision makers and sponsors know that you insist on better media for your children.

TIPS FOR GUIDING TELEVISION VIEWING

The tips below are from the Canadian Home and School Parent Teacher Federation. You're probably not going to incor-porate all of these rules, but if you pick and choose as if you are selecting choices from a restaurant menu, you will find that each choice chips away at television addiction and that your household members will gradually become selective viewers as a result.

- Decide if children can watch TV on school days, and if so, for how long.
- Determine how much TV can be watched on weekends.
- Be clear about the time a child can watch TV.
- Don't let children feel TV time can be saved up.
- Establish rules about finishing homework, practicing, reading, or doing chores before watching TV.
- Remind children that they have control of the TV. When a show is too unbelievable or scary, they can turn it off.
- Recognize that when a program is over, it is best not to just walk away. It is important to find out your child's feelings and impressions about the show.

- Keep in mind that specials may arise that your child may want to see. Such an additional show may have to be worked into the weekly allotment.

- Watch for children being captivated by habit-forming soap operas or serialized shows. There is little value in children keeping a daily appointment with such shows.

- Be aware that when children are alone, they get bored. Sometimes they turn on the TV because they're frightened. Parents need to offer constructive alternatives.

- Remember that just because a sensitive issue is mentioned on a TV show, it doesn't mean the show should be prohibited. If the program has merit, it may open discussion.

- Observe whether children watch TV even when they have friends over. Offer them something else to do instead.

- Ask yourself if TV-watching could be taking the place of activities that the family might do together. If the TV is on during breakfast and dinner, this suggests it is more important than conversation.

- Consider reading aloud to children fifteen minutes each day. Some studies have shown that time spent each day reading aloud to children inspires them to turn off TV.

WAYS TO COUNTERACT SECONDHAND VIOLENCE WITH YOUR KIDS

Parents can't prevent children from seeing violence on TV. However, you can explain why people do bad things to each other and/or their children as seen on television. Here are some suggestions:

1. Hug your children and tell them you will never hurt them or let anyone else hurt them after they have witnessed some terrible act on TV. Your child will become confident when he or she is surrounded by a strong sense of security.

66 Four out of every five parents believe pop culture negatively affects children. Single parents, especially, say they need outside help shielding their children from pop culture's emphasis on sex, violence, and vulgarity. 99

—Robert Maginnis, Family Research Council, Washington, D.C., 1996

2. Explain that most people are basically good. Only the weird, unusual ones get put on the news because what they are involved with is not ordinary.

3. Explain that some people are mentally disturbed and perhaps brought up by parents who had problems themselves. Again, this is not the case in your home.

4. Crime may seem prevalent because it is on the news, but a particular crime makes the news because it is unusual, not because it is commonplace. Explain that no such thing has happened in your town or neighborhood.

THE FOUR BEST WAYS TO LIMIT SEX AND VIOLENCE ON TV

Of all the influences of television, teachers talk most about the increase in children using sexual innuendo and solving their problems using violence. Cutting back on programs that expose children to one or the other is imperative if we hope to preserve our children's childhood. Taking the time to work through these issues with your children is a valuable use of time.

1. *Watch at least one episode of each of the programs your child watches to discover how violent they are.* When viewing together, discuss the violence you see, why it happened, how painful it was, how the conflict could have been solved without force. Explain how violence in entertainment is faked, not real. Encourage your child to watch programs with characters who cooperate and help each other.

2. *Choose TV programs with your child.* Just as you would never simply gather the family together and head out to the movies without having a specific film in mind, you should carefully consider at the beginning of the week which television programs you will watch and your children will watch.

3. *Limit viewing time.* Limiting viewing time has a dual benefit of not only limiting exposure to sex and violence but also forcing kids to find creative alternatives to the tube, such as playing ball, calling a friend, or going outside.

4. *Block out certain channels.* Federal law requires cable operators to offer a service that permits subscribers to block out channels they don't want. For families with young children, these might include channels that feature pornography and extreme violence.

MAKING TV A CHOICE, NOT A HABIT

To begin to change your children's TV viewing habits, enter into a simple dialogue with them, using these suggestions:

• Change their patterns: If your children want to watch TV,

have them ask you first. Just as they ask you if they can go out to play, agree that they must ask you if they can watch TV.

- Answer with questions: Don't just say "yes" or "no." Ask, "What do you want to watch?" Ask them if there's something else they've been thinking of doing, such as reading or playing outside.

- Ask yourself some questions: Is there some other activity that is better worth their time? Can I motivate them not to click on the set, but to involve themselves in something else?

- Start them on another activity: Take the time. Set aside what you're doing and get involved. Supervise the start of another activity. Choose a book together. Lay out the ingredients for the next meal.

These suggestions are not easy. In fact, they are difficult for the working mom and the busy parent. Don't beat yourself up if you can't always be there to change the course of events. These suggestions are meant to help you attempt to change the direction of your child's activity, if only for one day a week. Any step away from TV is a courageous beginning for you and your child.

BLOCK OUT COMMERCIALS

Remote controls may make us couch potatoes, but they also can be used to obliterate commercial messages. Get your children in the habit of blocking out sound during commercials. If they must watch cartoons or some other show, the bargain you can reach with them is that they must tune out the commercials.

TV RATINGS: A VIEWER'S GUIDE

You can use the television industry's rating system to help you choose which programs are appropriate for your children. The labels are as follows; the first two categories apply only to children's programs.

TV-Y, All Children. These programs are designed to be appropriate for all children. Whether animated or live action, the themes and elements are specifically designed for a very young viewer, including children ages two to six. Such programs are not expected to frighten young children.

TV-Y7, Directed to Older Children. These programs are designed for children ages seven and above. They may be more appropriate for children who have acquired the developmental skills needed to distinguish between make-believe and reality. Themes and elements in these program may include mild physical or comedic violence, or may frighten children under age seven. Therefore parents may wish to consider the suitability of such programs for their very young children.

TV-G, General Audience. Most parents would find these programs suitable for all ages. Although this rating does not signify programs designed specifically for children, most parents may let younger children watch such programs unattended. These programs contain little or no violence, no strong language and little or no sexual dialogue or situations.

The remaining ratings—TV-PG, Parental Guidance Suggested; TV-14, Parents Strongly Cautioned; and TV-M, Mature Audience Only—are not recommended for children.

Taking a Media History

Don't be surprised if the next time you take your child to the pediatrician a media history is taken—particularly if your child is there because he is hyperactive, apathetic, has injured himself doing something outrageous or violent, has trouble with his eyesight, or is experiencing nightmares. The American Academy of Pediatrics as well as the American Medical Association have taken note of the changing problems that today's children have, and are pointing the finger at television and video games. In treating your child for any of the above symptoms the amount of television he watches must be taken into consideration. The American Academy of Pediatrics is so concerned about the effects of television-watching on children that they have devised a series of questions and will use your answers to help them diagnose certain physical and emotional symptoms your child may have.

1. How do you decide what TV shows and movies to watch?

2. What are the rules about watching movies and TV in your home?

3. Is their a limit to how many hours are allowed per day?

4. Must certain activities be done before TV is allowed?

5. Do you eat meals in front of the TV?

6. Do you snack while watching? What do you eat?

7. How late do you watch TV?

8. What are the most watched shows in the house?

9. What did you watch yesterday?

These questions point up some of the problems that might exist in a child's television habits.

MEDIA VALUES CHECKLIST

Use this inventory to check your family's media habits when using video games, music, computer games, the Internet, movies, and videos. This is not a quiz; rather, it is a series of questions to help you check yourself about how aware you are of all forms of media in your children's lives, and has been adapted from an American Medical Association analysis of 1996.

Video Games Checklist

Do you own or rent games that have violent content?

Have you played the game so you're familiar with the content?

Is the game's range appropriate for your child?

Do you check the game's rating before you buy it?

Do you limit your child's playing time?

Music Checklist

Does your child have his or her own tape or CD player?

Have you listened to the music your child is playing?

Have you listened to the stations your child is tuning in to?

Have you talked to your child about the lyrics you object to?

Do you have age-appropriate limits on the types of music your child buys?

Computer Games Checklist

Do you own or rent games that have violent content?

Have you played the game so you're familiar with the content?

Is the game's age range appropriate for your child?

Do you check the game's rating before buying it?

Do you limit your child's playing time?

Internet Checklist

Does your child have access to the Internet at home?

Do you monitor computer use?

Have you investigated or purchased an Internet blocking device?

Have you found and listed child-appropriate sites?

Have you talked with your child about the best use of the Internet?

Movies Checklist

Do you make sure you know what movies your child is going to see at the theater?

Does your child need permission before going?

Do you check movie ratings before giving your permission?

Do you check movie reviews to know of the content and plot?

Do you allow your child to see movies that contain a lot of violence?

Videos Checklist

Do you own a VCR?

Do you monitor which movies your child picks out at the video store?

Do you check those movie ratings?

Do you consult other movie evaluations to learn about content?

Do you check with other parents about which videos may be shown at sleepovers?

Do you allow your child to see videos that contain a lot of violence?

THE TECHNOLOGICAL SOLUTIONS

As legislated in the Telecommunications Act of 1996, parents will be assisted in taking responsibility over what their children watch on television by letting the parents block shows with certain ratings through use of the V-chip. The V-chip is a piece of circuitry that regulates what can be seen on any particular television. The V-chip would allow parents to decide which shows can be shown on any television by automatically scrambling certain shows — for instance, any shows with the equivalent of an R rating. The V-chip is mandated to be an integral part of the construction of every new television set and therefore will allow parents (specifically single parents who are not always available to monitor their children's viewing) to protect their children from violence and adult content on TV.

Other proposed solutions are products called superVision and VisionLock.

Both of these products enable parents to set specific viewing times and maximum viewing allowances for each child.

TECHNOLOGICAL SOLUTIONS FOR COMPUTERS

Parental Guidance Plus, developed by Providence Systems, enables families to manage the cost and quality of their children's computer experience.

It enables parents to budget and control the family's use of online services, to monitor and limit children's use of video games and other programs, to review extensive-use reports, and to protect children and teens from adult-oriented Internet sites.

Success Stories

Staying unplugged is not deprivation. In fact, many families
report that after their decision to live without television, or with
a very limited amount, they feel free from the dictatorial hold
television had on their lives.

What follows are the stories of several families: the Eatons,
who never had television to begin with; the McKays, who followed the Four-Week No-TV Program; and the Rolfes and
Bennisons, both of whom participated in a no-television week
sponsored by their children's schools.

THE EATONS

The Eaton family had been living without television for almost
fifteen years when I met them. Hidden in the corner, under a
desk in the dining room of their home in Spring Valley, New
York, was a dusty old television set. It remained there on

purpose. At least three members of the family felt they were candidates for television addiction; they wanted the television completely out of convenient reach.

Chuck and Anne Eaton had three children: Claire, who was eighteen years old: Willie, who was fifteen: and Chandra, who was eleven. Anne taught music and English, and Chuck was a psychologist at Roosevelt Hospital in New York City.

"Television isn't a forbidden fruit," said Chuck, "but Anne doesn't believe in it for children, so when they started coming along, we had to make a decision about our viewing habits." The Eatons watched television three times in the year I talked with them. "We turned it on for the Super Bowl," explained Chuck, "and promptly the electricity went out. We watched the ball come down in Times Square on New Year's Eve, and I don't remember the third time."

Chuck arrived at this television consciousness by figuring out what television did to him. He would come home every night with papers to do. Anne, alone all day with the children, wanted to talk. The children also demanded his attention. In response to this, Chuck would turn on any old program and not do anything but watch aimlessly.

"I never liked TV, so it wasn't hard for me to stop watching," commented Anne. "And I felt it was wrong for babies to be watching. Have you ever really looked at a child in front of the tube? The poor thing looks like he's had the child knocked out of him. It's unnatural for a child, until he is about seven, to be anything but active and busy."

So rather than be done to, as Anne called watching television, the Eatons started doing for themselves. They kept a diary for a week to log the typical activities of a family who doesn't watch television. Heavy snow days had them all together for a few days in and out of the house. Two hours on Saturday morning were spent bird-watching. Outside, the children built snow forts, which ended up taking two days. The entire family went sledding and tobogganing. All the Eatons play musical instruments, so it seemed there was always some group or individual playing. Breakfasts and dinners were all sit-down affairs, with everyone together. Sandwiched between the fun were the weekly chores of bread-baking, food co-op work, Bach Society for Anne, Suburban Symphony for Chuck, baby-sitting for Claire and Willie, two sleepovers for Chandra, and a great deal of reading.

The Eatons were content with their life. "Let's say," said Chuck, "that at the end of the year I remember the concerts we attended, the people we met, and some shining family treks more than I would remember the television season."

THE McKAYS

Everywhere I looked in the McKay household in Pearl River, New York, there was a television staring at me. And yet, Edith McKay was determined to make her family more conscious of the television in their lives. The family methodically proceeded through the Four-Week No-TV Program; here's what they realized when they came to week four.

There are six McKays. When I interviewed them, two children were away at college, leaving fourteen-year-old Kathy and sixteen-year-old Tommy home with Jim and Edith. Jim commuted to New York City, where he worked on Wall Street, while Edith held down the fort, running a wild, busy household with a constant stream of teenagers coming and going.

Explaining week four, Edith said, "The house suddenly became very quiet, almost as if there had been a death or a good friend missing. We immediately resurrected several radios from the basement, and I got reacquainted with my favorite talk radio station."

Jim's preference was to listen to the radio news, anyway. He said his life was unaffected that first day until evening came and he automatically flipped on the tube. "No, no, Dad," reminded Tom. Jim settled down to a crossword puzzle.

Kathy McKay noticed one annoying thing during that first quiet week: her father's classical music. "Yuck!" was her comment.

"We all came together and felt closer," said Edith. "Everyone is in on everyone else's business when the TV is not there. That first week we observed the changes in our habits. I guess families tend to stop listening and watching each other if they always have the TV on. We were no exception."

"It is different, all right," chimed in Jim. "With less TV there is more midweek chauffeuring for me. Tommy cost me more money—the movies, visiting friends, and talking long distance on the phone."

"We started this experiment in the winter," said Kathy, "when I was always much more tempted to watch a movie or game show. Instead, now I get to clean out the basement, study harder for exams, chop wood, and shovel snow!"

She wasn't really complaining that much, her mother explained. "Her grades have improved immeasurably this term, and I think it has to do with Kathy's taking more time and being more thorough."

Edith realized that more free time for herself meant a newfound interest in creating some good meals. She also began to get out in the morning. "No dawdling over *The Today Show.*" Instead, she scheduled her paddleball game to a new early hour.

But there were some dismal times that first week without television. The McKays continued to pull out the television page from the newspaper to see what was on. One night Kathy saw an ad for a special and wished she could see it. In fact, as a sort of protest, she went to a friend's house to watch it. Jim was out of town one night, and Edith said she missed the tradition of the children gathering in her room to watch a few shows together. Instead, everyone was scattered. "Five o'clock was the grimmest," recalled Edith. "It's the time of day I least like, and I had always filled that gap with the news."

Initially the kids said they knew something else was missing but couldn't quite put their finger on it. Finally Tommy realized it was junk food. "We used to eat lots of munchy stuff in the evening. In fact, there were half-hourly gatherings in the kitchen when we used to all meet between shows to grab some food and find out what everyone else was up to."

"Now our hands are full of busy-type things—books, magazines, needlepoint, and projects," says Edith.

Kathy, a sports nut, doubles her time on the basketball court these days. She also reported sleeping longer and better. "I need more sleep than I used to get," she admitted. "Tommy and I have nothing to stay up late for, especially on Saturday nights, with the television control in this house."

Edith concurred and said she no longer gets a TV hangover. "You know the feeling, don't you? When you watch TV until you fall asleep. It can't be good for a restful night's sleep. I do sleep better now that the TV is out of the bedroom."

"We had always been a close family, but television was beginning to rear its ugly head," Jim said. "We were shutting each other out. We pick and choose carefully these days, using television after other possibilities are exhausted."

THE ROLFES

After several years of talking to and counseling parents on how to turn off the TV sets, I decided to go to the children themselves and began presenting no-TV week programs in schools. Many families' lives have been dramatically altered after their children participated in these programs. The children are enthusiastic and learn a great deal about a medium they once took for granted. In many cases their parents are less excited.

Some find that they cannot break their addiction to television. But many, with the help of their children, are beginning to try.

Life has changed dramatically in the household of Sondra and Trevor Rolfe since their children participated in a no-TV week program at school.

"We've cut out early morning TV altogether," said Sondra. Peter, who was seven years old at the time, had always been an early riser and had been watching television in the morning his entire life. "I never really approved, but what else was he going to do when the rest of the house was still asleep? But morning TV slowed him down; he was always dragging his body and was continuously late for school. Morning TV is something he chose to eliminate. In its place I get a little boy in our bed for a longer morning cuddle."

The most addicted member of the Rolfe household was Trevor, who agreed to go along with no-TV week while the children were up. The first night Trevor kept to his plan of no television until the children were bedded down. "The minute they were settled, the TV went on," reported Sondra. "However, on night two I felt a tiny sense of victory. After the kids were in bed, he opted for a book and conversation with me."

In an effort to convert their father, Peter and Allison, then age eleven, spent time after dinner tackling him on the couch, engaging him in conversation, showing him their schoolwork, and getting some reaction. "He didn't know what was happening," Sondra said, "but the kids were reaching out and Trevor was reciprocating." When Trevor did watch his usual dose of weekend sports, Peter and Allison would not go near him for fear of breaking their no-TV week pledge.

Sondra grew up in South Africa, and when she came to the United States, she was surprised and saddened that she seldom saw anyone outside, at least in the suburbs. Her feelings got a boost during no-TV week. "The street was full of kids, everyone doing something. The bikes were out, wagons were carting junk, basketballs were bouncing, Nerf football catches were going on on the front lawn. It was like a three-ring circus."

Sondra noticed that the neighborhood children needed one another more when television was out of the picture. "It was apparent to me that no-TV week brought kids together, both in spirit and physically. It brought the community out of the closet and into each other's homes. I don't want to sound Pollyannaish. Everything wasn't terrific. There was a lot of noise—excited kids, people coming and going, so much talk, talk, talking. Sometimes at the end of the day I longed to be just sitting quietly in front of the TV. Another problem, if you could call playing, talking, and the like a problem, was the mess. The children set up little retreats in every corner of the house. There wasn't a blanket or sheet in the linen closet. Once inside these little retreats, the children read, talked, played with their Legos and Matchboxes, and had fun."

One interesting note from the Rolfe household is that the children didn't gravitate to games. "They gravitated to each other and me," said Sondra. She was particularly excited about her daughter's newfound hobby: reading. Never an ardent reader prior to no-TV week, Allison was now reading frequently and choosing books to read to her younger brother.

After one week of no TV, the Rolfes learned that they definitely can live without television. The TV set had not been turned on by Sondra or a child for three weeks after the school program, except for one night. "I caught Peter watching a space documentary," said Sondra. "When I walked in on him, he jumped up from his seat and yelled, 'It's all right! It's all right! I've done all my work and this is a good, short show.'"

THE BENNISONS

"I only watched two hours of television last week," exclaimed nine-year-old Vanessa Bennison, as if she had accomplished a major feat. Vanessa's family had participated in her school's no-TV week, and as an ongoing project, Vanessa had pledged to watch no more than two hours a week for the remainder of the school year. In fact, all the members of the Bennison household felt good about themselves several weeks after participating in no-TV week.

Leslie Bennison, the mother of Vanessa and Dana, then five years old, was especially happy to see the trickle-down effect occurring with other family members. "Dana, our preschooler, is not a self-starter. With no neighborhood children in her age group, television had become Dana's best friend. During no-TV week, however, with her sister busy at projects and me generating play ideas, Dana began to leave television behind and gravitate to where the action was. TV seems no longer to be where it's at. I suppose the week was a real eye-opener in other ways," revealed Leslie. "An anti-TV program *must* involve the entire family. A parent can't just yell at the kids and tell them to turn the set off. I was forced to take a real position against television as well as take an active part in organizing everyone's time. At times I must have sounded like a broken record—'Get out those Magic Markers,' 'Build a castle.' The house sure looks different with little snippets of paper strewn around and paste stuck to the kitchen table, but there is also some maternal satisfaction."

The Bennisons were never what you would call an addicted family. However, Leslie was on the road to TV addiction when the girls were babies and her husband, Bill, was traveling half the year. "Back then I was watching TV day and night, slowly falling into a real trap. I began to realize that TV had a hypnotic effect on me, drawing me to it for no reason. Finally one afternoon I simply turned the darn thing off. I wasn't living my life anymore. I was living their lives—the television characters'!"

The big bone of contention in the Bennison household was one that exists in many homes: Bill Bennison had a sports addiction. "I must admit if I didn't travel so much I might be tempted to tune in to the ESPN sporting events every evening. Some of my male friends watch two or three events a night." In his defense he asserted that during no-TV week he probably clocked only two hours of sports. "On Friday night," he reminded his wife with a grin, "we were forced to do a real family number. It's rare that the four of us are ever together, alone. That night we popped popcorn and had wild games of Concentration and Scrabble. I found myself thinking how good it felt, the whole family around the card table."

Leslie thought that television makes men age a lot faster. "I think all the passive watching, especially for men, makes them sedentary and old-looking." No-TV week provided the perfect opportunity for her to chide Bill about his lack of exercise and lawn mowing.

Did the Bennisons' no-TV week provide any lasting effects? "Oh, yes, indeed," said Leslie. "We have absolutely no television now during the week. We are superconscious now of available extra time and fill it up with more productive alternatives. The other night, Vanessa finished her homework with ten minutes to spare before dinner. Instead of the easy out—TV—she went for a quick bike ride. Best of all, the house is calm. Even though there is increased activity, the noise level seems toned down. Everyone seems more relaxed, and I hope to keep it that way."

After a family begins to cut down on television viewing, a certain chain of events usually occurs:

1. The entire family will be forced to learn information— local, national, and international news as well as day-to-day trivia—from sources other than television.

2. Family members will also be forced to get their entertainment and pleasure from other people—family members, friends, and themselves.

3. The two situations above make for one very immediate result: more conversation.

4. The next surprise is more time—big blocks of free, unprogrammed time, which means less household tension and no hurrying of meals to make a program.

5. Lack of tension breeds breathing space—time to just sit and relax and perhaps linger over a conversation, happening, or special moment.

6. Lingering time means children who bask in newfound attention. Children begin to exhibit the first signs of relief that the television is gone.

7. Then what follows is a surprise for parents—the realization that their children know how to play and that parents don't have to be on duty programming play constantly.

Life takes on an entirely new meaning. With no electronic constraints, many free-from-TV families experience, for the first time, the joys of being themselves and of having the time to develop their own interests.

Bibliography

Books

Arlen, Michael. *The View from Highway 1*. New York: Farrar, Straus & Giroux, 1976.

Bennett, Steve, and Ruth Bennett. *Kick the TV Habit*. New York: Penguin Books, 1994.

Bettelheim, Bruno. *The Informed Heart*. New York: The Free Press, 1960.

Brazelton, Dr. T. Berry. *Touchpoints*. Reading, Mass.: Addison-Wesley, 1992.

Chen, Milton. *The Smart Parents' Guide to Kids' TV*. San Francisco, KQED Books, 1994.

Clinton, Hillary R. *It Takes a Village*. New York: Touchtone Books, Simon & Schuster, 1996.

Comstock, George, and Haijing Paik. *Television and the American Child*. San Francisco, California Academic Press, 1991.

Cuban, Larry. *Teachers and Machines: The Classroom Use of Technology Since 1920*. New York: Teachers College Press, 1986.

Deci, Edward L. *Why We Do What We Do*. New York: Penguin Books, 1995.

DeGaetano, Gloria, and Kathleen Bander. *Screen Smarts: A Family Guide to Media Literacy*. Boston: Houghton Mifflin, 1996.

DeLaMare, Walter. *Bells and Grass*. New York: Viking, 1964.

Elkind, David. *The Hurried Child*. Reading, Mass.: Addison-Wesley, 1981–1988.

——. *Miseducation: Preschoolers at Risk.* New York: Alfred A. Knopf, 1996.

——. *Ties That Stress: The New Family Imbalance.* Cambridge, Mass.: Harvard University Press, 1995.

Ellul, Jaques. *The Technological Society.* New York: Viking, 1967.

Gates, Bill. *The Road Ahead.* New York: Viking, 1995.

Gattegno, Caleb. *Toward a Visual Culture.* New York: Avon Books, 1971.

Goldsen, Rose. *The Show and Tell Machine.* New York: Delta, 1975.

Himmelweit, Hilda T., A. N. Oppenheim, and Pamela Vince. *Television and the Child.* London: Oxford University Press, 1958.

Huston, Aletha C. et al. *Big World Small Screen: The Role of Television in American Society.* Lincoln: Nebraska University Press, 1992.

Kenniston, Kenneth. *All Our Children: The American Family Under Pressure.* New York: Harcourt Brace Jovanovich, 1977.

Key, Wilson. *Media Sexploitation.* New York: Signet, 1976.

Lesser, Gerald. *Children and Television.* New York: Vintage, 1974.

Louv, Richard. *Childhood's Future.* New York: Doubleday, 1991.

Mander, Jerry. *Four Arguments for the Elimination of Television.* New York: William Morrow, 1978.

Mayer, Martin. *About Television.* New York: Harper & Row, 1972.

McLuhan, Marshall. *The Medium Is the Message.* New York: Bantam Books, 1967.

———. *Understanding Media: The Extensions of Man.* New York: Signet, 1964.

Means, Barbara. *Technology and Educational Reform.* San Francisco: Jossey-Bass, 1994.

Melten, Gary, and Carolyn Schroeder. *Big World Big Screen: The Role of Television in American Society.* Lincoln: University of Nebraska Press, 1992.

Moody, Kate. *Growing Up on Television.* New York: McGraw-Hill, 1980.

Murphy, Jane, and Karen Tucker. *Stay Tuned.* New York: Doubleday, 1996.

Packard, Vance. *The Hidden Persuaders.* New York: David McKay, 1957.

Papert, Seymour. *The Connected Family: Bridging the Digital Generation Gap.* Marietta, Ga.: Longstreet Press, 1996.

Pearl, David. *Television and Behavior: Ten Years of Scientific Progress and Implications for the '80s.* Washington, D.C., 1982.

Perlman, Lewis. *Schools Out.* New York: Avon Books, 1992.

Postman, Neil. *Amusing Ourselves to Death.* New York: Penguin, 1985.

———. *Technophy: The Surrender of Culture to Technology.* New York: Vintage, 1993.

Schramm, Wilbur, Jack Lyle, and Edwin Parker. *Television in the Lives of Our Children.* Stanford, Calif.: Stanford University Press, 1961.

Shade, Daniel, and June Wright. *Young Children: Active Learning in a Technological Age*. Washington, D.C.: National Association for the Education of Children, 1994.

Singer, Dorothy, and Jerome Singer. *The Parent's Guide: Use TV to Your Child's Advantage*. Reston, Va.: Acropolis Books, 1990.

Spock, Dr. Benjamin. *Rebuilding American Family Values*. Chicago: Contemporary Books, 1996.

Thomson, John. *Natural Childhood*. New York: Fireside Books, Simon & Schuster, 1994.

Toffler, Alvin. *The Culture Consumers*. New York: Pelican, 1965.

Wilkins, Joan Anderson. *Breaking the TV Habit*. New York: Charles Scribner's Sons, 1982.

Winick, Mariann, and Charles Winick. *The Television Experience*. Beverly Hills, Calif.: Sage Publications, 1979.

Winn, Marie. *The Plug-In Drug*. New York: Viking, 1977.

Journals

Aidman, Amy. "Advertising in the Schools: Selling America's Kids." Consumer Education Service, ERIC Clearing House of Information Resources, ED 389473 (1995).

Bandura, Alvert, D. Ross, and S. A. Ross. "Imitation of Film-Mediated Aggressive Models." *Journal of Abnormal and Social Psychology* 66 (1963): 3–11.

Centerwall, Brandon, M. D. "Television and Violence: The Scale of the Problem and Where to Go from Here." *Journal of the American Medical Association* 267 (1992): 3059–63.

Cohen, Dorothy. "Is TV a Pied Piper?" *Young Children's Journal* (November 1974): 4–12.

Dietz, William, M.D., and Victor Strassburger, M.D. "Children, Adolescents, and Television." *Current Problems in Pediatrics* (1991): 8–31.

Durant, Robert, Tom Baronowski, and Maribeth Johnson. "The Relationship Among Television Watching, Physical Activity and Body Composition of Young Children." *Pediatrics* (1994): 445–49.

Elmer-DeWitt, Philip. "On a Screen Near You: CyberPorn." *Time* (July 3, 1995): 34–38.

Flay, Brian, Stephanie McFall, Dee Burton, Thomas D. Cook, and Richard B. Warnecke. "Heath Behavior Changes Through Television: The Roles of DeFacto and Motivated Selection Processes." *Journal of Health and Social Behavior* 34 (1993): 322–35.

Funk, Jeanne B. "Video Games: Benign or Malignant?" *Developmental and Behavior Pediatrics* 13 (1992): 53–54.

———. "Video Game Controversies." *Pediatric Annals* 24 (1995): 91–94.

Halperm, Verner. "Turned-on Toddlers: Effects of Television on Children and Adolescents." *Journal of Communications* 25 (1975) 66–70.

Hayes, Donald, and Dina Casey. "Young Children and Television: The Retention of Emotional Reactions." *Child Development* 63 (1992): 1423–36.

Krugman, Herbert. "Brain Waves Measures of Media Involvement." *Journal of Advertising Research* (1971): 3–9.

Landau, Steven, Elizabeth Lorch, and Richard Milick. "Visual Attention to and Comprehension of Television in Attention-Deficit Hyperactivity Disorders in Normal Boys." *Child Development* 63 (1992): 927–28.

Leung, Alexander, Joel Fagan M.D., Helen Cho, M.D., Stephen H. N. Lin, and William Lane Robson. "Children and Television." *American Family Physician* 50 (1994): 909–18.

Postman, Neil. "TV's Disastrous Impact on Children." *U.S. News & World Report* (January 19, 1981): 43–46.

Reed, Sally. "Schools Entering the Computer Age." *New York Times*, April 25, 1982.

Sege, Robert, M.D., and William Dietz, M.D. "Television Viewing and Violence in Children: The Pediatrician as Agent for Change." *Pediatrics* 94 (1994): 600–07.

St. Peters, Michelle, Marguerite Fitch, Aletha Huston, John C. Wright, and Darwin J. Eakins. "Television and Families: What Do Young Children Watch with Their Parents?" *Child Development* 62 (1991): 1409–23.

Tonge, Bruce, M.D. "The Impact of Television on Children and Clinical Practice." *Australia and New Zealand Journal of Psychiatry* 24 (1990): 552–60.

White, Mary Alice. *TC Today* (Fall 1981).

Index